ROLE

A DIAGNOSTIC APPROACH TO PERFORMANCE

BRADLEY EMERSON

authorHOUSE®

AuthorHouse™ UK
1663 Liberty Drive
Bloomington, IN 47403 USA
www.authorhouse.co.uk
Phone: 0800.197.4150

© 2018 Bradley Emerson. All rights reserved.

No part of this book may be reproduced, stored in a retrieval system, or transmitted by any means without the written permission of the author.

Published by AuthorHouse 01/09/2018

ISBN: 978-1-5462-8713-1 (sc)
ISBN: 978-1-5462-8714-8 (hc)
ISBN: 978-1-5462-8712-4 (e)

Library of Congress Control Number: 2018900179

Print information available on the last page.

Any people depicted in stock imagery provided by Thinkstock are models, and such images are being used for illustrative purposes only. Certain stock imagery © Thinkstock.

This book is printed on acid-free paper.

Because of the dynamic nature of the Internet, any web addresses or links contained in this book may have changed since publication and may no longer be valid. The views expressed in this work are solely those of the author and do not necessarily reflect the views of the publisher, and the publisher hereby disclaims any responsibility for them.

Contents

Foreword vii
Preface ix
Acknowledgements xi
Introduction xiii

One: Role As It Is Played 1
Two: Skill And Knowledge Fctor 11
Three: The Attitude Factor 19
Four: The Environment Factor 25
Five: The Behaviour Factor 31
Six: The Performance Drivers 37
Seven: Performance 49
Eight: "Performance Roi" 55
Nine: Reward 57
Ten: Recognition 61
Eleven: Progress 67
Twelve: Responsibility 71
Thirteen: Growth 75
Fourteen: Excellence 79

Conclusion 83
Reviews 85

Foreword

Disruption has and will continue to fundamentally change the way we live and work. Today's society including businesses, government and individuals are responding to shifts that would have seemed unimaginable or unthinkable even a few years ago. Today we are working in a workplace that is characterized as increasingly volatile, uncertain, ambiguous and complex (collectively known as 'VUCA'). Artificial Intelligence (AI) and Robotics are reinventing the workforce and will continue to impact the workplace for many years to come. Drones and driverless cars are transforming supply chains and logistics resulting in enhancing the quality of life. The way we live and work is about to go through a profound change. For some countries, this has already been happening for quite some time now. The rapid advances in many technologies are expected to continue disrupting many of the industries in the various economies, and the impact will be felt across the globe.

These social, economic, and technological changes increasingly lead to a discontinuous and fragmented career context in which transitions occur more frequently than ever, hence there is a critical need for employees today to examine their individual roles within the organizations they served. Research has shown that there are several factors that would impact and influence an individual's career mobility or progression. As an employee, it is crucial to be able to partner with your managers about your career aspirations and identify areas that you may wish to improve or develop, as well as identify and request for the resources required to do so.

As an employee you should have a well-defined job description and understands the skills and competencies you must develop in order to progress up the career ladder. You will need to set aside the time and flexibility you need to complete learning and development activities while at the same time ensuring development is having an impact on performance.

This book on 'Role Diagnosis' by Bradley Emerson provides you with a Framework that would examine every role or job position will demand 'performance' from the perspective of the employers or organisation and it is important for you as the employee to understand as to how best to perform your role with the end result of meeting our employer's expectations and anticipate that you will be rewarded as an outcome of this.

On a final note, it is worth to reflect on the Quote in the concluding Chapter by the renowned Olympian, Usain Bolt, who is arguably the fastest man in the world who said "When I was younger, I always wanted to impress, to be good for my country, to make them feel good, and sometimes that meant I didn't focus on myself enough. I learned I had to put myself first. And it's fine because I want for me the same thing that they want for me, which is to win." This means that you would need to focus on your purpose and aligned with that of your organization and this will result in the success in your job acceleration of your career.

Prof Sattar Bawany
Chairman & CEO, Centre for Executive Education (CEE Global)
Strategic Advisor, International Professional Managers Association (IPMA UK)
Adjunct Professor, Curtin Graduate School of Business, Curtin University, Western Australia.

4 January 2018

Preface

It was sometime in mid-1994 and I was attached to Commercial Bank of Ceylon, Head Office, as Senior Manager Operations, when I received a memo from the HR department nominating me for a training programme at the Indian Institute of Management (IIM), Bangalore. Little did I realize that a lunchtime conversation with Prof. Agrawal, who was the course director, would result in a book, twenty years down the road?

It was a one week training programme and Prof. Agrawal made it a point to join the participants for lunch at the restaurant. More importantly he sat at different tables on each day to ensure his casual engagement with all the participants. The day he joined the table I was seated at, he asked me this triggering question: "What do you want to achieve in your current role?" I didn't expect that, hence took a few seconds and said that I want to make an impact; to leave a "never before and never again experience" with the people I am working with and the customers our unit was servicing. And then came the lines that provoked me and impacted me throughout my working career.

Dr. Agrawal said, "Bradley, in my long years in training I have come across many young managers who had very similar aspirations. And it is not unusual that all these managers, whether from the private sector or public sector, have their roles prescribed. When you work to a prescribed role, you are in a restricted territory, and it's very unlikely you will bring the role to life. You need to diagnose the role if you are to bring the role to life. Then you can make the impact you want to make".

This handbook is an outcome of twenty plus years of pondering, searching, researching and training on the subject.

Thank you Prof.Agrawal for planting the seed.

Acknowledgements

Accomplishments, big or small; is an outcome of supported efforts of many. I want to first to thank the inspiration and guidance from above and to my children for they have sacrificed their time with me, in support of my maiden effort to convert my thoughts to a book.

The model you find in this book is out of my learnings, experiences and convictions over the last fifteen years of my work life. The examples I have referred to are a collection of lasting experiences created by wonderful people I had the good fortune of coming to contact with. Overall I want express my gratitude to me colleagues at Commercial Bank, Bank of Oman Bahrain and Kuwait (Muscat, Sultanate of Oman), Nations Trust Bank, Pan Asia Bank, CIMA (UK) and the Public Private Partnership Unit of the Ministry of Finance, Sri Lanka to have given me the experiential learnings that have been briefly captured in this book.

I thank the work and support of Dorothy Lee of my publishers, Author House, 1663 Liberty Drive, Bloomington, UK, Buddheepa Ratnayake, who designed the cover and young journalist Vinavie Gayara who patiently, spent time listening to me and converted my thoughts in to words. My thanks also go out to every single person who encouraged me all the way from the start to the end.

Introduction

Prescribing work to people dates back to 3500BC, to Egyptian, Roman and ancient Chinese times. It ensured their administrations worked effectively. People were expected to religiously follow a procedure every day. In early modern times this system came to be called bureaucracy, and it was formalised to ensure consistency and efficiency. By the middle of the 19th century, industrialised nations found this system very useful for maintaining consistency in output when using less literate labour. Most management books give credit to the German sociologist Max Weber as the first to endorse bureaucracy as a requirement to thrive during the industrial revolution. There is evidence showing how the trend gained momentum through the 19th century, spread from governments to large organisations and was firmly established within the 20th century.

In the mid-1800s Karl Marx viewed that while corporate and government bureaucracy seem to operate in opposition, in actuality they mutually rely on one another to exist. He wrote that, "The Corporation is civil society's attempt to become state; but the bureaucracy is the state which has really made itself into civil society."

However most of the management literature of recent years positions Weber as the first to formally study and popularize the word bureaucracy and hierarchical organization and relate it to the chain of command, division of labour, organizational rules, assignment of tasks and a method to complete complex administrative tasks and so on. Given the skill levels of the short supplied labour and speed of industrialisation Weber saw bureaucratization as the most efficient and rational way of organizing human activity. Over time however the intellect and intelligence of the labour improved and found bureaucracy to be a threat to individual freedoms, caging the individual's potential through rule based rational control.

Prescribed job roles still exist today, and they will continue to exist in the future. Organisational structures and hierarchies have changed to accommodate multitasking and multi-functional teams. There is much more delegation and freedom to people now. Labour has over time become workforce to resources to human talent, giving importance to talent. To me talent is simply: "competence and the confidence to demonstrate that competence". Whether at the start of the career or through promotions and progressively higher positions there will always be "Job Descriptions" (JDs). We all know that people with the same JDs end up with different levels of performance. There can be many answers to the question 'why such disparity?' More often than not, external factors will be cited as the main reason. However, we all know external factors may not be the main reason for the performance disparity. External environments have always been dynamic, and we need to be able to shoot a moving target. In a dynamic environment when performance is prescribed, we end up limiting the "talent".

Can we expect a free for all work environment? No, for sure! A prescribed work environment is a reality, though the degree of rigidity may differ. Yet, do we allow our "talent" to corrode due to rigidity? Employers, managers, departments, colleagues and team members are not permanent. We, ourselves are "permanent" and therefore nurturing our talent becomes our sole responsibility. Performance as per prescription will not bring out your best in a role, not when compared to a diagnostics approach. The challenge grows as we move on from that first appointment and we progress higher through promotions, be they within the same company or in another. Often we are promoted to new roles based on our performance in the current and in the belief that we would deliver similar performance in a new role. Moreover, the promotions find someone to fit an existing role rather than looking at what the role can evolve to be in a dynamic business environment. Do we now see the gap?

In this handbook, I have endeavoured to bring to you a simple model that will help you to continuously take a diagnostic approach to your role, which will enable you to stay ahead of the pack, always. Enjoy the read.

Bradley Emerson

One

ROLE AS IT IS PLAYED

"Every day we choose who we are by how we define ourselves"– Angelina Jolie

Work life for many is 'life', and can be as long as life can be. During the journey of our careers we have a natural desire to progress, and most of us will. Some very quickly, some at a slower phase. Historically progress is seen by us and society at large as a move up in position. This progress could either come from within the company you are in, based on the company's requirements or you could outrun the company's time line and join another in a higher position. Your career journey could see you in different positions, geographic locations, different industries and different companies. You will have various designations, with different responsibilities as you go along.

Take a case of two young people from the same school, same qualifications; join the same organisation, as starters in the same job with the same enthusiasm and aspirations. Five years down the line, we are very likely to find one person ahead of the other. What do you think made the difference? Let's find some logical reason for this question as we read along.

We all know that every position will demand "performance": We believe if we "perform" our role, we meet our employer's expectations and we anticipate that we will be rewarded. The counterpoint to this is: What demands do we set for ourselves? How do we measure our performance in relation to personal development? And how do we reward ourselves? The primary question is: Is there a difference? Or should there be a difference?

Within our careers we try to portray a role but we mostly fail to fit into it as we don't understand what feels good, what looks good nor do we understand the satisfaction we gain through a good delivery as we fail to convert our expectations. This is primarily due to the extensive focus given to the organizational objectives and organizational goals which control and govern the actions of the organization. However, as humans, as professionals, one's personal goals and objectives should be in line with the company's objectives in order to deliver a stellar performance.

For example, suppose an actor plays a role of a villain and through dialogue and cruel behaviour he or she would portray the role so realistically that the audience ends up hating the character. That's what is expected from an actor. To do that, firstly he or she will have to transport to the villain's world, often symbolized by a dark and dangerous setting. He paints a picture in his mind with thoughts of the darkest night with the moon hidden behind the clouds and the massive castle covered with creeping vines, surrounded by bats and the ghosts of his world. Then he or she would visualize the story of the villain. In most cases this would be his lonely childhood where he was ill-treated, which inadvertently moulded him to be the malefactor he is now. Finally, the actor incorporates in to the villain's character the evils of the world defined by Pandora's Box such as envy and hatred to portray it perfectly. Is this the definition of a talented actor?

Players in the business world spend their everyday lives on perfecting the art of the work they do (hopefully) within the circle of work life **(fig. 1)**. Yes, it is a circle of limitations, circle of expectations and a balancing act of external expectations to internal capabilities. This is what we dive in to every day to carry out the given tasks.

An example, persuade customers to buy their products/services. They repeat this cycle, day in, day out. It is also the case with a stage artist, who is contracted to perform in the same play and in the same role. The actor, day after day, scene after scene brings his role to life. Players in the business world spend their everyday lives on perfecting the art of the work they do (hopefully) in their (perceived) role, within the circle of work life *(fig. 1)*. Yes, it is a circle! It's a circle of limitations, expectations, and a balancing act of external expectations to internal capabilities.

However, most of us, no matter where we are in the organisation, do not pause to think of what exactly are we doing when we work, our role and the impact it creates to ourselves, to the business and the society as a whole. This is where often people lack as they tend to underestimate themselves and be pressurized to the extent of having influenced behaviour. Unlike a stage actor, the "role" is not defined to our potential and to reward ourselves for what we bring out. This sense of discouragement is rife within the business executives today. As you read on this book you will realize how important the job you are doing right now is and how it matters to yourself in a holistic sense. This knowledge should serve as a simple form of encouragement to enhance the spirit of a progress minded person. Whenever some say to me of "career mindedness" I decode it as "progress minded". The role in a business is the part that the employee plays to *enhance oneself* and help achieve business goals

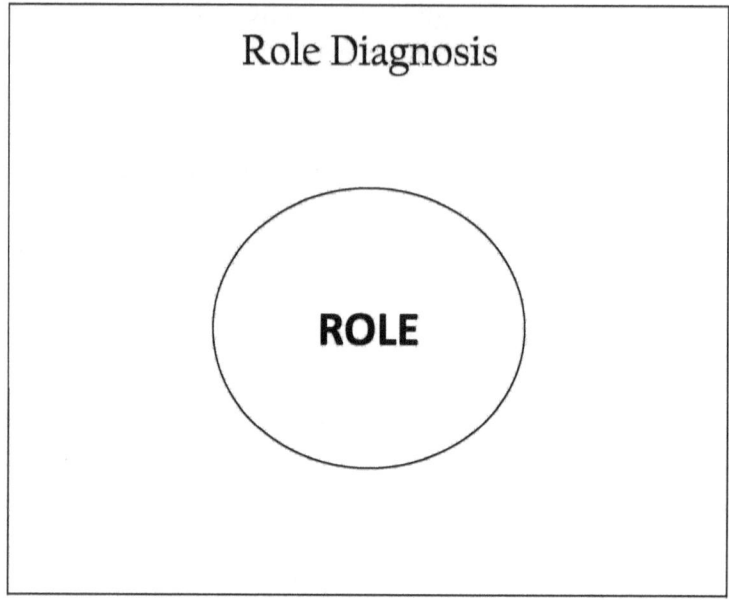

Fig 1

Enhancing oneself ideally should precede the engagement to the role. What happens in reality is that we try to enhance ourselves on the job. In this way, are we not training while running the race? Have we all not heard of the phrase, *"On the job training"*? Sounds ridiculous isn't it? Yet, that's what we most often do. Can you imagine how unprepared we are for the job and how much both the company and ourselves would have lost out? This situation exists within companies because we put ourselves up based on what we have learnt, not so much on how we have applied our learnings; our experience from times in the past where the situation, circumstances, resources and our abilities were different.

Typically a role at work would represent the daily functions of a position of employment and in most cases, one's role interpretation is clouded due to the influences and the environment that exists around which will be discussed in detail. The word 'role' is defined in the dictionary as the function assumed or the part played by a person in a *particular situation.* Now, we know that different roles have different situations and therefore your capabilities need to be diagnosed to best fit the situation, and the situations change constantly. Don't we often dive in with the same skill (or experience) without sharpening what is needed to meet a specific situation? Is this not why we all love this line *"fire fighting"*.

Understanding or rather diagnosing the role is crucial in a job because it affects behaviour and performance and these two aspects, although they are summed into simply two words can decide your whole career. A person taking up a new job will be introduced to the business's vision, mission and their inspiration. The business will have a set of goals that they strongly work towards. Even a new business will be started with the aim of reaching great heights and these will be broken down into objectives that can be measurable within a certain time period. This is common knowledge. When these objectives are being met, the business is on its way towards achieving the ultimate goal. This ultimate goal not only means the company's vision, but moreover the personal vision of the one taking the job. A person will take an opportunity not simply because he wants to achieve the goals of the business, but with a benefit for himself to grow. Most take up jobs to support life rather than to discover the purpose of life over time.

Often we are asked the question of 'where do you see yourself going in life?' In this book however, I would encourage you to answer the question 'How do you see yourself in five years?' Framing the question this way can help you work towards achieving milestones in your career and further your dreams. Therefore, defining the role is not limited to aligning it with the business objectives. The role player has to carry it out in a way that helps him or her be who he or she has the potential to become. Aspirations may help to meet the full potential. This is a difficult task. Most adults in this generation tell millennials that success can be achieved through hard work. Working hard towards your goals will help you greatly, however hard work done blindly without analysing your environment will burn you out (aren't we all at the end of each day?). How you should behave and portray your role will only keep you in the same step. On the other hand, understanding how your role should be played to benefit your goals as well as the business goals will help you in the long-term to reach your potential and to be competent.

Mintzberg's managerial roles give an idea on how to be a competent manager, where you constantly switch roles to adjust to the situation and to the task at hand. For example, being a spokesperson will require that person in the role of the manager to sell the product and even the business. The manager will represent the business to outsiders and here the manager's role is to act as a salesperson for the business, to convince and to create interest. Another role is being a disturbance handler where the manager has to take charge when problems occur and act to resolve them. This shows that a person is not limited to one specific role in a job. It has to change when the situation requires you to. A person who knows when and how to change their role accordingly will be skilful at their job.

Think back to the actor who portrayed a villain. That is how the world perceives a **role**; a specific stereo-type that is "expected" to be carried out and change is the unknown. A villain is expected to be the one who creates havoc, the killer, the betrayer and the ultimate loser of every battle. Bollywood actors are amazing unlike the Hollywood actors. In Hollywood you can name the heroes and the comedians. In Bollywood one person can fit it to almost all roles and bring them all to life.

Our minds have been poisoned by society to believe on a fixated idea that history has built along the years, and the environment has to match in accordance. These occur because we have been brought up with ideas such as that a villain is evil and cannot be made to change and we should earn to be successful. This is where most of us are wrong. We often have a misconception of the role we are playing in our daily lives. We live in the delusion that a role has to always be defined for us, (though, invariably it is so). It is almost robotic that we handle this role every day without questioning why we do so. In a world of self-driving vehicles and platforms connecting millions of people together, we are still unaware of the impact a role can create or rather expected to create; thus, we still remain loyal to the delusional role we are taught; we are still hesitant to re-define it.

People do not often spend time understanding and more importantly *reasoning* the role of a job. Our lifestyle is such that we are expected to perform outstandingly in the designation that we choose and there is a prescribed or a historical function that we carry out which we plug ourselves into to perform. Reality check- This, however, does not help you to fulfil your maximum potential. It is human nature to underestimate ourselves when performing our job role, but our potential is far greater than what we think. How do you get to know your potential? If a talented actor's personal objective is to simply put on an act on stage and not to do an Oscar winning performance he would fall short of fulfilling his obligations to himself as an actor, and would give a half-hearted or blind performance disappointing the audience who would have had high expectations from him. The actor is not one who only portrays the villain as evil, but one who manages to deliver the story. Although it is embedded in our minds that villains are up to no good, it is the presence of evil that reminds us that there is hope to overcome. They help us create a story and they can impact lives for the better. Most of us tend to be too pessimistic and therefore we trap ourselves in a box filled with a false imagery of roles during our career. Millennials have to start defining themselves outside the box and to be self-aware of the position they are in. This will help people to reach their potential and be not just satisfied, but truly happy at the end of their journey.

Marriage – A Compelling Example

Let me take a simple daily life example to elaborate the core of this book. Consider the "role change" of a girl getting married. Who or what do you think will influence her role? Firstly the girl will have a broad idea of the role created by various influencers based on their own beliefs and judgements. Primarily the husband to be will have an expectation although he may not share it with the bride to be. (*If he did the marriage might be a risk...hahaha*). From the girl's own family and in-laws to the extent of culture and religious background will define her role. In particular, her husband with his great expectations will be a major influence factor for her character. He will expect her to change her pattern of living, which can be defined as her new role in life. What happens in society is that we are clouded by the noise of family expectations and this tends to influence our role in the most unimaginable manner. This is because the role that we take up is with the focus of what we want to do as opposed to who we want to be. We have always been secluded to a finite number of options and we've been told that if only we perform on these options, we are able to be successful. As open-minded people, we should never settle with influence. However, influence helps us take wise decisions. It should help us broaden our options. But we must never allow it to change who we are. The woman herself will have her own conviction based on her religious background, family, culture and media which would be her perception of the role that she should be carrying out when she becomes a wife. This can be the character she has paved in her mind from her childhood that she wants to fulfil now as a wife. There will be a point where this will differ to the other's expectations, creating a gap that ravages the woman's mind, causing her to misinterpret her role.

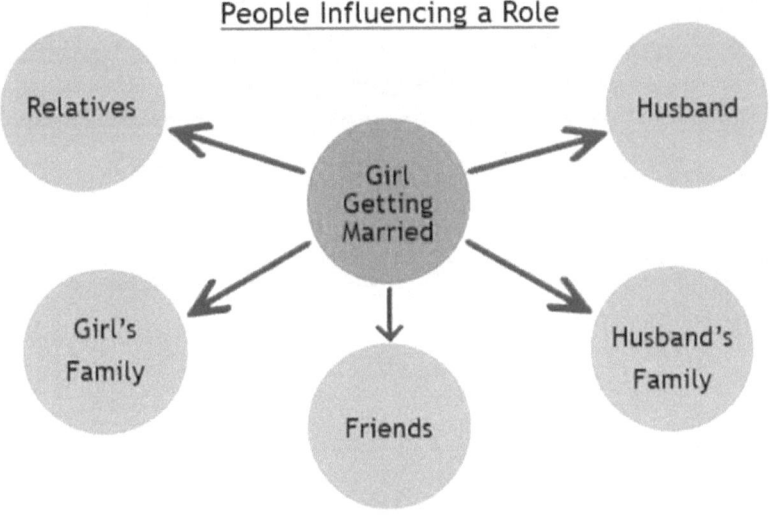

Fig. 2

How different is our work role compared to the example of the girl who gets married? What defines or rather influences the definition of your role at work? Primarily your line manager, your predecessor, staff, peers, people in the same role in other companies, your family, circulars, instruction manuals, so on and most importantly how you yourself has defined the role in your mind are the influences.

Whether it be the girl who is getting married or you at your workplace, there will be external expectations that will be influencing you. These expectations are really their own definition of the role which they want seen in you. There are fair reasons and rationales that may have evolved through their experience and expectations. If you ask people to define the role of a doctor, you are bound to get varied responses. These responses are really what one expects the role to be.

Two

SKILL AND KNOWLEDGE FCTOR

"Skill is the unified force of experience, intellect and passion in their operation" – John Ruskin

For a role to be performed well it requires skill and this skill comes with practice and commitment towards the job. Let me pause here to ask a question. Let's go back to the girl who was getting married. What skills do you think she would have developed to perform as a wife? (Female readers who are married will have a long list to reply with). Of course don't men acquire a set of skills after marriage?

Skill is basically the ability to do something well and to become an expert at it. Even a job as simple as folding tissues requires a certain degree of skill and we must understand that this is obtained through time and a conscious effort. The skills that you gain have to be constantly and consciously improved and failure to practice will result in you losing the skill you have. Therefore, it is important to know that the world today moves very fast and the skills that you have acquired at one point of time will become ineffective unless they are enhanced.

The skill therefore is a self-equipped ability to do something in an above average way and helps develop the individuals in performing a role. A person joining a new job will be influenced by multiple perceptions as to how a job needs to be done. This unfortunately is different from "how a role needs to be performed". What would be the difference then? Simply put, *job is functional; role is vocational*. Hence, they develop the notion that they must learn the skills required to perform the already established way of doing the job. However, using a person's skills to initiate and conduct the job in a greater way creates a difference and a new stance to the job is what is required to succeed in the latest way of being successful in business.

Skills are measured in this era with the education you have, how many degrees you obtain and the job experience you have. Finding jobs in this time is quite difficult due to the competitive nature of people as everyone who applies for a job has a degree nowadays. What employers fail to notice is that skills do not depend on the number of degrees you have or how educated you are, it is how you carry out the job you have been given and how dedicated you are to perform the tasks.

Skills are *not* measured in this era with the education you acquire, how many degrees you obtain, the book knowledge and the job experience you have. There are many we will come across on the streets with amazing skills.

Role Diagnosis

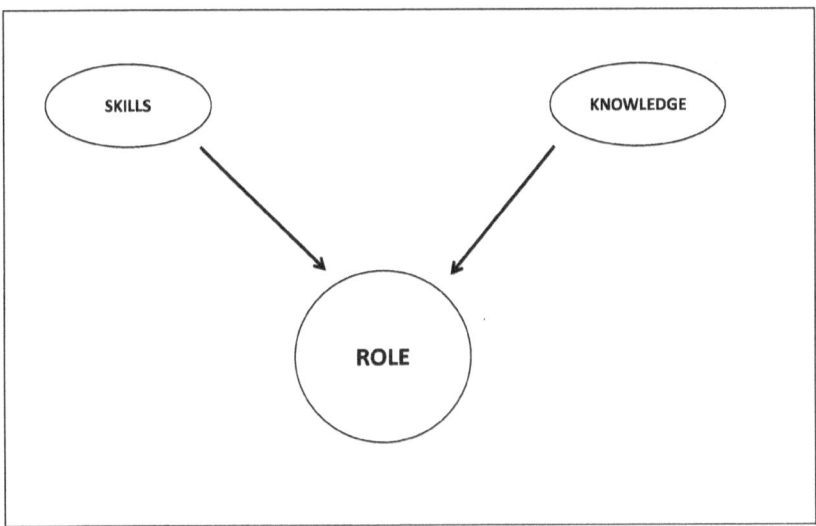

Fig. 3

How education helps enhance the skills is when one can find the relevance of the learning to a skill and apply that learning. Similarly, how experience can help to sharpen the skills is only when one can unfreeze from the clutch of experience. We all now know that the fast changing world of work is making experience obsolete. As the saying goes "what worked then won't work now". However, experiential learning is also knowledge, therefore, as in academic learning; it needs to be applied to keep the skill relevant.

Sun Tzu explained the acme of skill as using your knowledge to "win-all-without-fighting" which means that one must practise the right use of one's skills at the right time. It is necessary to analyse the possessed skills before you use them to perform your role. The right use of skills will help you become recognized for good performance. In the present age, for most working people, one career throughout their whole work life is not a possibility. It's more so noticeable in their first ten years of work. They will switch to different jobs, more than to gain experience in various fields, but to find the fit – to see what really ticks them.

The knowledge factor: Here I am not referring to education based knowledge. In relation to role diagnosis, to enhance performance the knowledge required is beyond education. One needs the academic knowledge no doubt, but don't forget that there are many cases of managerial failure due to the absence of role related sensitive knowledge. Let's go back to our heroine – the girl who is changing her role to a wife. What do you reckon the role related knowledge would be? (No prizes for the married ladies who answer this). Whether, she moves in with the in-laws or not, she would need to understand the power structure within the family, the level of acceptance of her husband, the culture and the communication styles within the new family and also the culture and beliefs within the family. All married women reading this will agree that the spouse is not a sample of the family. And if by chance our heroine is the second wife, then knowledge of the previous wife and her relationships with the family may also be required. Obviously our heroine cannot send out a questionnaire to the family, but needs to learn to pick up form behaviours and indirect signals.

Similarly, when you move in to a role, be it by appointment or by promotion, you need to acquire "role related" sensitive information. One needs to get to know the power base and more importantly the line manager's fears and challenges. At one point of my career in the banking industry, I was transferred to the largest branch of Commercial Bank of Ceylon outside Colombo to head the operations. Just before I left, I met with the Managing Director Late Mr Edgar Gunatunge, Deputy General Manager Mr Daya Pitadeniya and AGM Late Mr Randolph Silva. I was told that my transfer was part of the plan to revamp the branch management. I still remember very well the words of Mr Pitadeniya – "Young man, you might find it difficult vis-a-vis the old management styles of the incumbent manager. But don't throw in the towel, better grind your teeth and wait until the changes are complete" The location was totally new to me and the only person I knew in that branch personally was the one I was replacing.

When you go with such an expectation from your higher management your biggest challenge is to win the confidence of the very senior branch manager. First thing I did was to call the person I was replacing and ask him what his biggest challenges were and how the present team got on with daily affairs. The frustrations he came out with gave me the impression, "you are the culture" – This, however, can differ within departments even within the same organisation. Knowledge of the prevalent culture of the place is critical for you to get a grip of the ground situation.

Knowledge is said to be power, that includes the knowledge of the terrain you are about to embark on. Knowledge we normally refer to and rely on to perform the role is gained through years of education, experience and learning. Knowledge and skills determine your strengths (in your mind) when you apply for a job. You, when you are recruited, you believe that you were picked for the job because you have the necessary knowledge and skills. Reasonably so. Also, you are hired because the employers had the same belief, and reasonably so. What happens in reality is that we set off to apply our existing knowledge to the new role that we have to perform. Have you not heard of people saying "in my previous place"?

In the event of you start as a manager, you need to have a thorough knowledge of your team. Start with a one to one conversation with your team within the first two days. Three questions you must ask during this conversation:
1. Why do you think you have been placed in this department?
2. Have you been able to apply your full self to the role you are performing? (in my long experience almost everyone answered "NO" to this question)
3. What prevented you from applying your full self?

These questions will give genuine answers because, the members of the teams also want to give it a new start every time the boss changes, but invariably don't get that chance. In 1992, I took over the Travel Department at Commercial Bank Head Office as the Senior Manager. And during my 'three questions' conversation I came across this young lady officer who said that she didn't even have a said task. She was more like a substitute waiting for someone to come off the field. I could see the spark and the burning desire in her eyes, waiting for the baton to be given to her. And I did, and she ended up heading the unit as the Senior Manager. The conversations revealed that the twenty odd people were awaiting to be unleashed. Imagine, when you unleash the desires of such people they help you bring their potential to life. In 1992 and in 1993, the Travel Department became the benchmark department of the Bank. This is the "knowledge power" that I am talking about which will bring your role to life.

Each team member is "activate" in a different way although everyone has the ultimate intention of being noticed. The knowledge or rather *intelligence* about your team is critical for you to bring your role and their role to life.

"A small team of A+ players can run circles around a giant team of B and C players" – Steve Jobs

Role Diagnosis

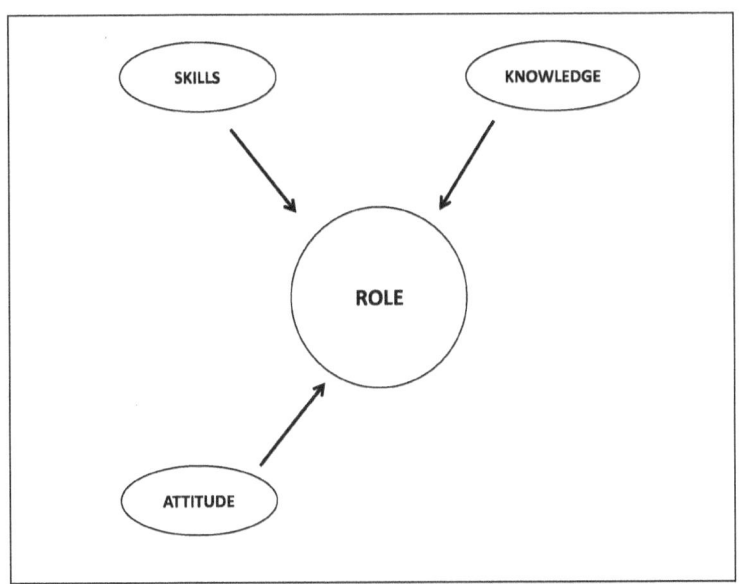

Fig. 4

Three

THE ATTITUDE FACTOR

"The way you start your day will determine how well you live your day" – Robin Sharma

'Hire for attitude, train for skill' is the new norm in recruiting people today. How we perform our role will depend on our own attitude to ourselves, our workplace, and individual and collective attitudes of others. Attitudes influence and are influenced. Attitude has become critical to fit in a role as there are more and more people who have lost jobs due to attitudinal issues rather than to competency and knowledge issues. Therefore, we need to be conscious how attitudes can change even as we progress in our careers. For example, when we become managers, we are vested with more power, given a bigger office, a company vehicle and other perks – all these will have an attitudinal change. Not necessarily, only at work, but may be also at home and in the neighbourhood. This is quite human.

Attitude is easily one of the most spoken about traits in the personal development space. According to Wikipedia, attitude is an individual's *predisposed* state of mind in relation to a value and it is precipitated through an expression (or non-expression).Since attitudes reflect what's deep rooted in an individual, it comes out more honest and consistent than our words and actions, which disguise the real us. Therefore, in different situations, "attitude" can either be your best friend or your worst enemy. Having said that, what is attempted in this chapter is to draw attention to recognizing the attitudes in defining a role. Consider our heroine, the girl who is getting married – would she not pre-empt a few attitudinal changes to the existing ones or will she contemplate on a new set of traits even before getting in to the role of a newly married spouse? This is where all those expectations come in to play.

Envision a situation where you have just received a promotion. You then go through a phase of change in your mind, shaping yourself to the new role. Preparation for the particular new role is likely to be based on the role of the previous person who worked in this position. And subconsciously we tend to assimilate the attitudes of the predecessors. But this would be simply like getting in to someone else's jacket. We often do this and end up as a misfit for the role and naturally so.

Take an example of the flight stewardess. Leaving aside her inherent attitudes is she not expected to craft new attitudes to suit the role? This is where I want to take you. When we take on a role, do we consciously ask ourselves what attitudes would I expect from this role? How would I expect myself to feel when interacting with someone in the role that I am about to take on? Attitude is key to bringing any role to life. Different roles will have different attitudinal requirements and mind you the role perceptions are dynamic. Isn't it then critical to diagnose your role in terms of the required attitude that will make you relevant to the role?

As I said earlier, attitudes are influenced and are influential. The Dalai Lama pointed out that we are in a world with wider freeways but narrower viewpoints. We have taller buildings but shorter tempers. Will Smith explained that we spend money we haven't earned on things we don't need to impress people that we don't like. Thinking out loud, this is because we are often too lazy to adapt to our roles, to be the change or to make a difference.

We want to be a good wife/husband, mother/father, a good supervisor, a good manager but we do not want to make the effort or to dare diagnose the skills, knowledge and attitudes consciously to make these to happen. We for sure enhance the skills, knowledge and attitudes as we go along, but in careers, learning on the job may be costly.

It is perplexing how each of us can build up our own definition on the way to be "good" at our role by acquiring knowledge, skills and attitudes that define the role and of ideas regarding the role.

Our roles begin with perception, the way we and others view our role. Perception will reflect the outcome. Internally, we must believe to bring justice to the role we play. Certain questions that help strengthen the perception on the role to be performed are imperative to the role-players to do a "good" job.

We have been focusing on what influences the role and where does it come from? This can be deduced in a scenario of an employee attempting to understand his role in order to perform right, leave aside, exceptionally. We all know, and as we have discussed, an employee is defined by the circular processes that is present in a framework in which you have to commit to in your role. An influence that is often neglected or given less attention to is market perception, which is the assumption of the customer and their impression on what you perform.

Technology has become mandatory in our daily lives, one that we cannot live without. We are able to witness a constant stream of media consumption among the youth today and this has led to a huge and most importantly a negative impact on the way youth performs their role and their perceptions of reality. Market perception influences the way we see what role we play in society. The media culture that we live in is such that it can create a load of flowery, sometimes even be the source of lies and rumours. Nevertheless, don't they impact the attitudes of a role? The attitude of a marketing manager for example is largely affected by media although one who is smart will use this to his advantage. Media makes products seem magical, triggers judgement, creates attraction and is the reason behind many successful businesses at present. The marketing manager would choose mass media for promotion and he can use advertising to aim at the target market. Similarly, how the manager deals with the media itself has an impact on how he performs the role.

All the influences combined will be technically and in ritually exposing the person to a circle of expectations. If this expectation is not being met, people form an opinion in their minds regarding their disappointment of your poor performance compared to their expectations.

A role will be influenced, however this can be balanced by the attitude that the person has towards the role. The attitude that one develops towards the role they are taking will affect the performance as well. If the employee is promoted to a role that he once dreamed of, the attitude towards the role will be a positive one and therefore he will be motivated to work hard. Therefore it is important to understand the impact of personal attitudes towards the role. There will be excuses and slacking if the person's attitude towards the role is not aligned, even it has to be self-imposed.

In the movie "The voice of God", Morgan Freeman discussed in the Hollywood Reporter on the roles that defined his career. He explained the role he had to play as a real-life high school principal in the movie "Lean on me" by saying that if you want to portray a real life person, you need a lot of emotional input from them. In contrast, he also had to play the role of "God" in the film "Bruce Almighty" where the role could not be defined compared to the movie of a real-life person. Nevertheless, he is an actor with the power to make us cry and make us love. Understanding the expectation of the role was a crucial part of his success in every emotion that he made us feel, through his transformation for the character by giving life to it.

Role

In contrast, the practice in a workplace is quite different as most hectic lives of workaholics revolve around promotions, designations and responsibilities and they do not stop to review the role and what effort they can take to make their performance of the role distinctive and unique.

It can be understood that a new job role requires expanding your knowledge to perform the role, enhancing skills to suit the job role and an attitude change. With these changes being done, the next step is to mould your behaviour accordingly.

Four

THE ENVIRONMENT FACTOR

In most work situations, there is usually more to see than what meets your eyes. A lot happens just beneath the surface"
- Abhishek Ratna

There is a significant difference between "designation" and a "role". Designation is how a position is identified; Role is what a position is expected to deliver Disney's employees are known as "cast members" for the various roles they play of the Disney characters in a day's work. Prior to the employees dressing for their roles, each cast member understands the role that he/she has to bring out in respect of what is already in the minds of the visitors, or audience. The importance of understanding the character, every behaviour, look, feel, walk, talk, etc., etc. and demonstrating them all through the shift, brings to life the role that is portrayed. Like an actor in different movies and stage dramas, it will mean that they have to understand each different role that they have to play and depict the role perfectly.

A "loud hall" with the sound of a music band banging through the speakers and into your ears will ease your tension and create the mood where you feel relaxed and pumped up at the same time. Although it is difficult to describe, the environment and your surroundings affect you. This is no different to a workplace where a free environment will spread positive vibes and motivation, (or the opposite) where it will allow employees to explore their creative minds. This partially depends on the environment that an employer creates within the organization. But more on what each one creates for himself or herself. The environment involves the influences made by external forces which affect your job role and you and your intent in a major way.

This can be validated in the context of our heroine, the girl, now getting used to married life. Influences will now surround her decisions and choices. Various influences and judgements from the family and in-laws to the extent of culture and religious background will influence the environment. In particular, her husband with his great expectations will be a major Influence factor for her character. He will or may although untold, expect her to change her pattern of living, which can be defined as her

Role Diagnosis

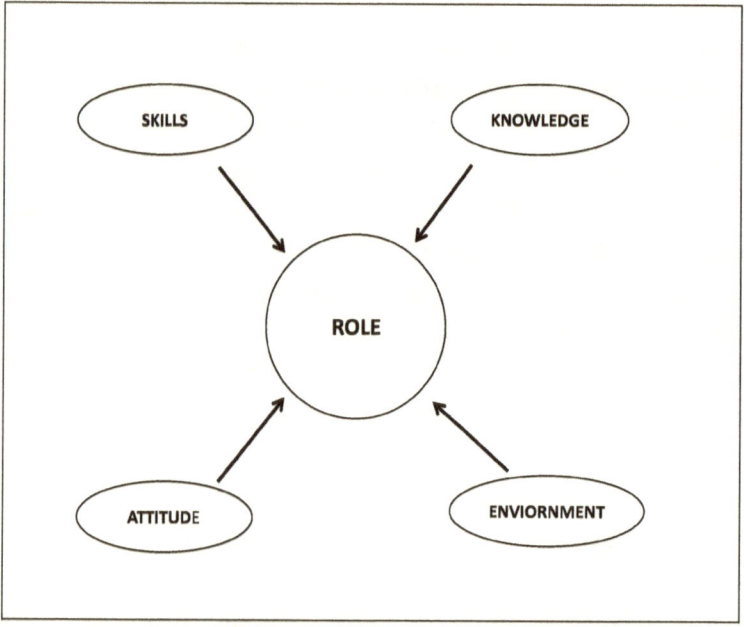

Fig.5

new role in life. (Same goes for husbands). What happens in society in our part of the world in particular is that we are clouded by the noise of family expectations and this tends to influence our job role in the most unimaginable manner. This is because the role that we take up is with the focus of what we want to do as opposed to who we want to be. We know for a fact that we are who we are, given the environment of a moment or a situation.

We have always been exposed to a number of options or constraints, and we've been told that if only we perform on these options, we are able to be successful or are perceived to be so. As people with strong individualism, we may resent or tend to ignore environmental influence. Take for instance a performance that lasts less than ten seconds, the men's 100M dash. Performance will depend on the altitude of the track, humidity and temperature in the stadium, the wind speed and direction at that moment and those others on the line with you. Sensitivity to such environmental influence helps the athlete broaden the options to manoeuvre his performance.

What is your typical work environment? Isn't it made up of the location of the office, how you get there, the look and the feel of the office, the ergonomics, lighting, collective energy, the level of delegation, freedom, processes and procedures, and your customers? Don't all these collectively and individually impact your role performance each day? Should we not be conscious of how we will react or maintain stability in performing our role regardless of changes to one or many of those factors? Try to recall the times the start of your days was messed up purely by external environment factors?

One time in cricket, sledging was a big part of the playing environment and Aussies are quite notorious for this specially during the "Ashes" against England. This is to unsettle the batsman even before he starts to perform, and continues to distract him with regard to each and every ball he has to face. Over time batsmen learned to either to be totally insensitive to the comments or more so learnt to give back the fielding side in return. This is the best as per Google, when Sir Ian Botham walked in to bat, Rod Marsh, the Australian wicket-keeper asked Botham "So how is *your* wife and *my* kids?" Sir Ian Botham replied, "The wife is fine, but the kids are *retarded*". And then focussed on the game. Our own Arjuna Ranatunga and Kumar Sangakkara are also known to respond with equal wit. This apart, the playing environment will also come from the pitch report and the weather report that are considered even before the final eleven are named.

The reason I picked these elaborations is to emphasise how most of us ignore the impact of the (changing) environment to our role. There will be variations in the environment as you move up the ladder even within the same organisation. When running a business or performing a role within the business, there are stakeholders who influence or even put pressure on the environment through their expectations. Mark Zuckerberg, the founder of Facebook was belittled by his stakeholders as they urged him to sell the business. This led to a misunderstanding and a blur of different views and opinions of what the decision should be and Zuckerburg had a choice on how he would perform his role in this situation. Nevertheless, he believed in what he was doing despite him being alone as one by one his management team and his stakeholders gave up on him. He refused to live up to stakeholder pressure but instead followed his own belief of his role.

Back to our heroine. The role of a wife or for that matter married life is a very challenging one, especially when raised in a different cultural environment. This results in numerous new actions of judgement and traditions that need to be followed. This is yet another influence on the role of a married woman (or man) as she must respect the culture and adapt to the surroundings of her family as she aims to be someone her new family is proud of. The world matures in different ways to different people or the different roles they have to play and adapt. The newly married woman or a newly promoted manager can choose to perform the respective roles in their own way, whilst being conscious of the environment. Being insensitive to the environmental influences to a role would see you as a victim of it. Just rewind your careers. See how many instances you have been insensitive to the changing environment and given a second chance, the role would be played in a completely different way.

In the fast-moving world, the way we work is significantly changing. Structures, designations, reporting lines, peer pressures are significantly getting altered. The positions we are in will be subject to the changes mentioned above. You may have already experienced it or are currently experiencing it. If not you will soon. Diagnosis of the role is therefore required to bring the role to life. As opposed to this, what most of us do when we change roles by getting promoted is to continue almost the same way, a glorification of the previous role. We are hesitant to unfreeze the behaviours of the previous role and identify and diagnose the new role, totally from a clean sheet basis because *your new position is not an extension of the old position.* Accept that when your role changes, your zone changes and thus we have to break out of our comfort zone of your previous role environment.

Breaking inherent "instincts" that have been put in place for years is not easy at first, but we have always defined ourselves by the challenges we have faced. We are often held up by sticking to our status quo vis-a-vis the previous role that we carried out that we become resistant to creative and uplifting change when our role alters. Workers in the modern world must be quick to adapt to change and break out from their comfort zones to perform an outstanding role. Oh, by the way, in my opinion, "hell" is another word for comfort zone. This process takes effort as it requires a diagnosis of the zone, a complete analysis of the new zone that the employee is involved in will enable the worker to gain an understanding of the "role" and help him execute the role in a higher quality.

In the game of cricket, which I referred to earlier, before the match begins, it is beneficial to determine the behaviour of the pitch. This will enable you predict what to expect (predictive analytics) and perform according to how the pitch will behave. Analysing the game thoroughly by identifying the bowlers' strengths, your opponent's weaknesses and diagnosing the playing field is the start to a competitive game. By understanding the behaviour of the pitch, you can adjust yourself to suit the environment so that you can give a good game with the role you play as a bowler or a batsman.

Businesses today is becoming digital, driven by innovation and run by individuals in the new generation who would be challenging systems and broadening paths. This is the attitude of the incoming generation who would change the work environment. There are open-offices and telecommuting and youtubers making videos within the space of their rooms and making millions and travel bloggers who are paid for simply sharing what they love doing. This is the generation of entrepreneurs and "curing cancer", it is time we challenge our roles.

Be like the Millennials. They are those who threaten the existence of a repeating role. They will as the role-taker, create a definition of the role for themselves. This, however, can be applicable to an extent, because in some jobs the experience of the previous person and following his or her ways may be beneficial to help learn the job, but it need not be to play the role.

The thinking out loud started from Albert Einstein when he said that *"The problems we have today cannot be solved by the same thinking we used when we once created them"*. We need to diagnose and define our role differently, in the process of researching alternative ways to execute our roles. The definition of the word "good" tends to differ with each individual. Some are satisfied by simply doing what they are told (living by prescription) and others want to make an impact by diagnosing the role and bringing such roles to life.

Five

THE BEHAVIOUR FACTOR

> *"That human behaviour is more influenced by things outside of us than inside. The 'situation' is the external environment. The inner environment is genes, moral history, religious training"* – Philip Zimbardo

A new role, be it a promotion, or a new job, leads to a change in attitude as your mind is overwhelmed by the power which drives into you. This changes your actions, not simply at work but even in the home surroundings. This effect mainly occurs as a job role changes to one with higher authority and status. However, a change in the job role will not immediately result in an improvement in your performance. As it was discussed earlier, a new job role will require a change in attitude, enhancement of skills and expansion of knowledge to suit the job role and the recognition of the environment in which it is performed. With the above changes in yourself and the changes in the working environment, firstly your behaviour in the new job role will be moulded accordingly. *We begin to behave the new role before we begin to perform the new role.* The influences of behaviour in a job role are the perception you have on the role, the expectations of others, the skills, attitude, knowledge you acquire and the response given to you regarding the job role you carry out. The challenge that is faced by most working minds is when does this behaviour become performance? We all know clearly that at the end of the day it is not the behaviour that is recognized but the performance that is expected from you.

You know these promotional videos that hit your inbox, where the promoter of a product goes on blabbering for about ten minutes of the features, how the other users have benefited and then you saying in your mind, *"get to the point"* and you end up fast forwarding the video or exiting from it. Career roles are the same. People are waiting for you to get to the point. What is that point where behaviour becomes performance?

In any game of sports players are required to perform and therefore need to learn how to convert behaviour into performance -to perform the expected role. Simply changing your behaviour according to the job role is the initial natural thing to happen. But it will not replace performance. We often question as to why we are not being recognized for "performance" when what we do is simply behaving according to the role. Therefore, we need to have an understanding of the difference between behaviour and performance.

Behaviour is defined as the way in which one conducts oneself, especially towards others (or towards one's job). Your behaviour on a job can also depend on the experience you have gained during your career or in the case of the first appointment, the perceptions. An organization has different categories of employees who succeed in being productive in their own unique ways. A theory that supports this would be the two types of employees that McGregor described as X and Y. One employee would work when they are given financial rewards whereas the other is motivated by non-financial elements such as empowerment, recognition and responsibility. The question is how do we identify the different drivers that transform people from "behaviour" to "performance?" Managers need to carefully observe the behaviour and the role of each of their subordinates. This can be most relevant in the case of a role of a sales person. A sales person deals with customers as an employee. By depicting their character, it is easier to categorize them and identify how they can be motivated.

Considering the McGregor's theory, type "X" employees can be identified through his or her behaviour. There are also the types of employees who have a negative notion towards themselves, work and are lazy. They require constant supervision and do not elude any liking towards their quality or quantity of output, yet are seen to be "engaged". This is more due to a misfit that results from poor role diagnosis. Behaviour can be identified by observing how employees carry out their daily activities such as responding to a problem, handling customers and talking to peers. Employees give out signals by their way of action and reaction. This is where one needs to pause to evaluate the cause for such behaviour and address the root cause. Once your personal signals are understood by yourself, it is easier to recognize if you are behaving or performing. In my long managerial experience, I have had many people complaining to me that they work hard, but they have not been recognized.

The next question that arises is how is behaviour important in a role? Behaviour affects your performance or rather preambles the performance and thereby your role. Behaviour and performance are two different but dependent aspects that significantly have an effect on each other, day to day, in the role one plays. Organizations are changing their way of dealing with people's behaviour as today's factory worker is literate, intelligent, and more sensitive. Factory workers now have the authority to suggest ideas and change ways of how the production line works.

Role Diagnosis

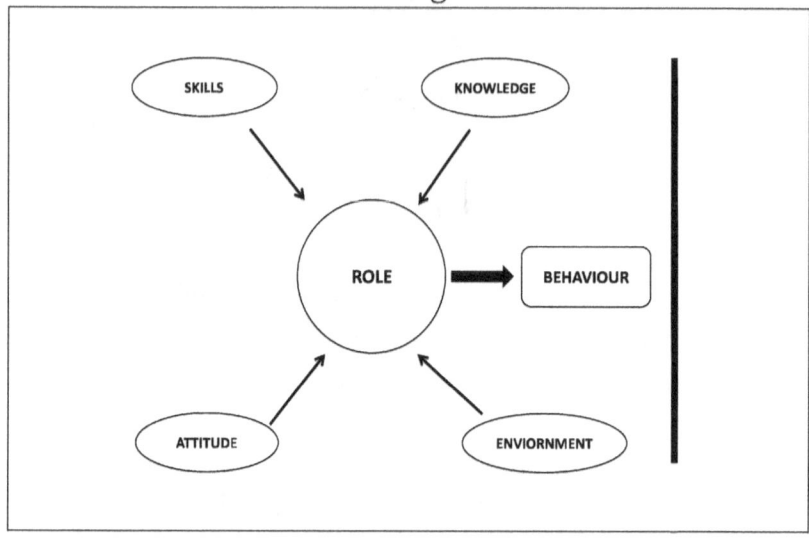

Fig.6

A sales person should behave in the right way to attract the customer - be professional and respectful to the customer. Yet this is not performance but contributory factors to performance. His or her sales tactics should be used in a subtle but effective way to get the customer responsive before getting interested. The behaviour of the salesperson can solely determine whether the sale can be made or not. This is a strong example of how behaviour affects the performance in a role. Roles are usually differentiated according to behaviour. The behaviour of a manager is different to that of a factory worker. These two roles require different behaviour. A factory worker should work according to the instructions given and reduce errors whereas a manager overlooks the operations and takes decisions. Nowadays most of their defined ways of behaviour have been threatened and behaviour in organizations is changing. It is important to keep in mind that behaviour affects your performance. However, it does not have to be limited to the role you are required to play. Your inherent behaviour can be different to what is expected from you. Your way of working maybe different but as long as you are positive that it is suitable to the role and will improve your performance for the better, it is worth behaving in your own way.

Once when I was with Commercial Bank, there was this senior teller, who during his annual appraisal said that he has over ten years of experience and that the bank has not promoted him to a staff officer grade. He had not taken any banking exams because the bank did consider experience as a criteria for promotion. So I asked him what experience he has gained in the ten years other than counting cash. The answer was that he was the most accurate, never had cash shortage or an excess in his entire career. So I asked him 'you have been accurately counting cash for ten years. Is that the experience you want the bank to recognise and promote you?' Grinning, he said, "of course Sir". What I told him after that he said he never forgot in his entire career. I told him "to be a cashier in a bank you only need to be able to count to ten accurately, and that's all that it takes to pay and receive cash without a mistake. If you want the bank to promote you the bank needs to benefit from your experience at a higher level. How will the bank benefit from you counting up to ten accurately for ten years? You have been thinking attendance is experience, it is not. Most importantly if you work like a dog, you will be treated like one and you will have only yourself to blame. Go, look for opportunities to engage and add value to the entire cash management operation in the branch. Then you can claim you have experience". Most of us think attendance is experience, unfortunately it is not.

Each role that we may take up in our work life will start with us behaving on the role. Behaviour is not performance. The question is where the line between performance and behaviour is? For some it can be a line, for some it can be a hurdle, for some others it can be a wall. Whatever it may seem to be it has to be overcome. So read on.

Role Diagnosis

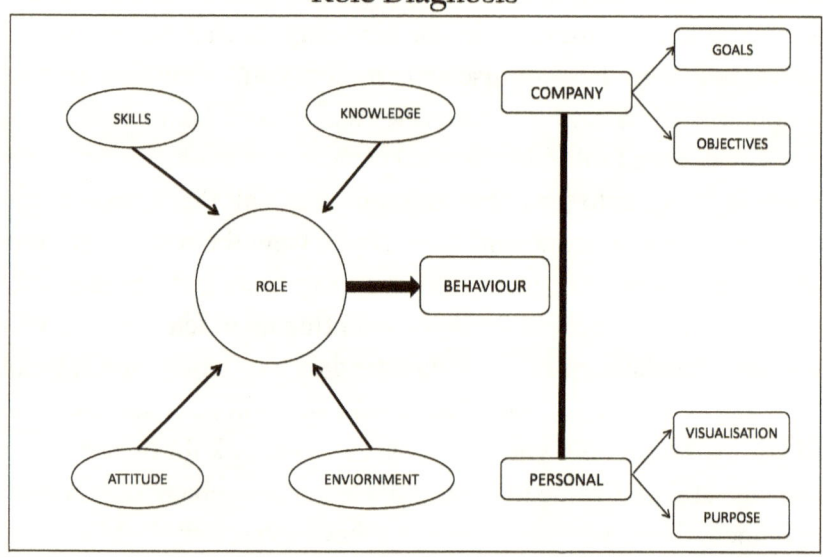

Fig. 7

Six

THE PERFORMANCE DRIVERS

"You don't get cited because you are conventional, you become a model because you went against the conventional wisdom and prove that they were wrong you are right".
Lee Kuan Yew, Parliament speech on November 1, 1994

Behaviour in a role comes from conventional influence. When Lee Kuan Yew set out to establish Singapore he did not choose to be driven by conventions. Performance in a dynamic business environment will outplay those entrenched in conventional wisdom who will find their way to the backburner. To leapfrog from behaviour to performance and sustain the same, one needs to understand the correlation between the company purposes and self-purpose. A company has its short term objectives and long term objectives. It is true that we are primarily hired to meet the company's objectives, but I want you to park that for the moment and bring forth the notion of what is it for you. The reason I want to divide the focus at this point is that, however compelling the company's objectives and goals may be, you could put up a good show only if you can visualise the role you have to play and the purpose thereof.

Role Visualised

Have you ever imagined yourself owning a large group of companies that are globally recognized? You speak loud and clear to a large audience as a successful entrepreneur. Or have you even envisioned yourself owning a small cosy boutique, one *that represents your personality* and something that you have always wanted to share with the world. Whether it be that large company or the smallest boutique that you dream of starting, it is your visualization of what you want to become in that situation which is important. Your visualization will affect the way you would initially behave and how you conduct your role. Moreover, it will be a compelling case for you to acquire the *skills, knowledge, and attitude* required for the role. When you are given a job, visualizing how you are seen to be doing it will drastically determine your performance. We don't usually do this. (Neither did I in the first two decades of my work life). You create an image of yourself and the unit you are attached to, big or small, how you successfully handle your role. This is the starting point for converting behaviour to performance. Visualization can be similar to a boxer hearing the sounds of a killer punch and the sound of an opponent crashing on the mat. Visualisation could be like feeling the finish line ribbon touching your chest.

Take the example of an athlete who gets selected to take part in the 100M sprint. Is he or she not running for himself or herself and when he or she puts up a winning show does the country benefit? No doubt he or she has the national flag in mind but more so they visualise themselves winning. It is the same with any sport. It is the personal mastery that comes first. That's why one sweats out on the track, in the gym, or on the court.

Even a company itself has its vision where it might hope to become the leading business in the market it operates in and hopes to be the best at what they do. Take Apple for example. When Steve Jobs started the company in the garage, he visualised where the company will finally end up. His marketing mantra was, "The consumer does not know what he wants until we tell them". Visualization is an advanced state of imagery for both the company and an individual. Companies have visions, but individuals need to visualise if they are to move from behaviour to performance. It helps you visualize what you want, out of the role you play, and this exists in the short term for a particular role. Visualisation is stronger than the dream, because you feel the reality.

How does visualization help your role? An actor visualizes a scene before playing it out. He is given a role to play and he imagines how his character has to be portrayed in the particular scene, and it is with this visualization that he lives the role in the scene by making the visualization a reality. Even when you consider a play for instance, the director first visualizes how he wants the scene to be and this is the foundation on which he decides the characters, costumes and props. Visualization can act as a driver in anything that you do. Likewise, in your career you visualize the person you ought to become in a particular role. This visualization is a conscious process but gets recorded in your subconscious mind. Where do you visualize your "performance" and "the outcome", rather than the "perception" of the "role"? This subconscious personality may have been moulded throughout your childhood years from your passion and changed with influences. It starts at the age of six when your teacher asks you what your ambition is. A little girl may say I want to become a teacher and a boy might say I would like to become an engineer when I grow up. When you are six years old, you say this because you are often subject to gender biases. As the children grows older they begin to self-discover their passion but often over ridden by parents or by society. However, the passion to do whatever we want to do comes out. Nonetheless, this is why we have engineers becoming bankers, doctors becoming businessmen, business graduates becoming "moccasins", whereas school dropouts like Bill Gates, Mark Zuckerberg and Steve Jobs become who they are.

The "person that you want to become" is built over the years and it remains in your mind with each step that you take. When you accept a job, you visualize how you would play your role to help build this person in your subconscious mind. However, there is always a gap that will prevail between the person you are now and the person you visualize yourself to be. The difference can sometimes be a weakness in you as you become unsatisfied each day due to the gap. Let's assume that a person takes on a "marketing manager's" position in a company and he visualizes himself leading advertising campaigns worldwide. He builds his own storyline and thinks of the role he plays. Once this image is fixated in his mind, if he performs less or differently he will feel that he is not living up to his potential. This will create self-doubt and this is a main cause of demotivation for a person, especially when leading a team. It will lead to work stress and the manager over-working himself. Ultimately, he will realize along the way, he will become someone better than whom he visualized himself to be! So, you might say then what is the purpose of visualizing the role that you are to perform?

The answer is that by having an image in your mind as to what you want to be, it will subconsciously begin to shape you and push to pick up skills, knowledge and the right attitude and even to seek guidance and to become self-activated. Self-activation is higher level of self- motivation. Although it can be flowery, your mind is your most powerful motivator and having a visualization of how you could conduct the role successfully is a method that could improve your performance of the role.

Role Purpose Personalised

In sports one trains with personal purpose to ensure a great show. I remember listening to Susanthika Jayasinghe, 200M silver medallist at the Sydney 2000 Olympics and then the fastest woman in Asia. She was saying that during her training in the USA, under Tony Camble she used to fall flat on her back fagged out after sprint training. Tony, she said would walk up to her, pull her up, and say, "Let's walk Susan". And during the walk he would ask her, "Susan, don't you want to put up a good show? Don't you want to win an Olympic medal? Don't you want to beat Marion Jones? Don't you want to bring tears of joy to the eyes to you parents? Do you want to make 20 million people of your country proud? And Susanthika had said yes, Yes, YES louder and louder visualising every situation and restart to sprint. This is the impact of visualisation I am talking about that drives a winning performance.

There will be days where you ask yourself, what is my purpose? How can I impact this world for the better? Each level you accomplish and each step you take from your childhood to your education, your career and in life itself, you will search for a meaning and higher purpose. To convert "behaviour" to "performance," you need to ask, "Why am I here(?), especially when taking up a new role.

At the start of your first job you might think that this job will help you find your purpose. Then you might think that you just needed to get a few promotions. You might wake up each day looking for something new but at the end of the day you might find yourself where you started. Purpose is much larger than money, recognition or validation. It is something that you do for yourself and builds in yourself that keeps you going. Once you discover your higher purpose, your role would unveil itself and it will give you the necessary motivation to wake up each day to work harder. What can be a person's higher purpose? What will drive you to push all your boundaries and overcome your obstacles? What will help you succeed in every role that you will play? How will you serve the world? What do they need that your talent can provide? Arnold Schwarzenegger said that "when you work for something greater than yourself, you find meaning, you find purpose". It is up to you to find the impact you can make for others. Once you find this, it will improve you and your performance enormously. However, our minds are designed to feel motivated to do the things that are easy, but when it comes to taking a step ahead, we seek for a higher purpose to do so. You are sitting at a meeting and you have an incredible idea and instead of saying it out, you hesitate. What none of us realize is that when you hesitate at that micro-moment, it can stop you from being the person to make an impact. It can keep you from realizing your higher purpose. It can stop you from taking a step ahead to work towards your purpose. Whether you are a doctor who is powered to save lives every day or even a hotel steward who serves others, a purpose exists for you. You have the ability to change the world, even in the smallest and simplest way you can and once you find that way it will help your mind to stop hesitating. It will help your mind to let out your ideas at that board meeting without any hesitation. It will help you to prove someone wrong or go that extra mile to serve another.

How does purpose fit your current job role? Your company has a mission, which is broken down into several objectives and further into targets for each person to achieve. You are expected to work towards achieving these objectives in order to determine the success of your role performance. However, if your personal purpose is not fitted into the company objectives, your role fails. Your purpose has to match the company's objectives in order to be directed in the right direction. If, however, the business objectives and your purpose are worlds apart, your focus will be different and it will benefit neither you nor the company. But when a higher purpose prevails in your mind, you are not limited to the company's objectives. Company objectives can change over time and the goals you are given to achieve may change as a result of a promotion, transfer or a change in job. It is important to diagnose the role and how it aligns with your purpose to ensure enhanced performance.

Your role is determined by two factors, your personal factors and company factors. When devising the role of a job, both these factors are significant and help characterize your role. Your personal factors can be what you hope to achieve with this role and how it can mould your career. Company factors can be the goals and objectives of the business and how your role plays a part in achieving these.

The Company Perspective

Let's now go to the question we parked at the beginning of this chapter. If you look at *Fig. 7* you will see I have drawn a line or rather a barrier before you move from behaviour to performance. Behaviour, we now know, becomes performance only when the outcomes appear. It is also now clear there are company perspectives and personal perspectives for outcome. We have dealt with the personal perspective focusing on visualisation and purpose. Company or corporate goals and objectives are determined by the headship and approved by the Board. The management develops the strategies and puts in place the structure to execute the strategies. Now this, you will find in any management studies. What I want to focus more on is how the alignment of company journey to your career journey will impact your performance. The two journeys may not sync, in the long run, but what is important is optimise the opportunity at that point of time. It is like you having to attend an interview. You take a bus, and if the bus is likely to be late to get you to the destination you will get off the bus and take a taxi. The biggest mistake we make is to sit in the bus, hoping you can give an excuse. Remember excuses are given to yourself before you give it to another.

Corporate Goals

Goals we know are long term, and are often privy to a few in the company. Not even the annual report will detail such for fear of competition getting to know those. Nevertheless, the corporate journey will be directed to reach that destination. As junior managers you should make an effort to find that out. Your midyear review or the annual review is the best opportunity to find that out. I as a senior manager did that. I made it a point ask my manager three questions during by annual review and the discussions of my KPIs for a particular year:
1. What are your KPIs and what are the top three things that will make your show look good this year?

2. What are the three most critical outcomes for the company this year?
3. Where does the company want to be in terms of revenue, balance sheet growth and market share?

This might sound radical to most of you, but ask, you must. Without knowing that there is no way you can shape yourself to bring your role to life. Remember you are in the payroll to help your boss put out a good show and make your department, branch, unit, to look good.

Most of us find ourselves in a struggle which is known as the "knowledge - action – outcome gap", although we sometimes may not realize or admit it. We get trapped in a reality where we often know what to do, but which we cannot seem to make ourselves do. We have incredible ideas, but each day we are compelled to hit the *snooze* button. As Mark Zuckerberg said, "Ideas do not come fully formed, they only become clear as you work on them. You just have to get started." We keep things that are relevant to company goals in our minds. We have the necessary knowledge about everything we want to do, but our minds hesitate. Aligning yourself to the company goal can help you beat your brain. When you are purposeful in your role to deliver company goals, then you have an intention on something that you want to change about your work life and it registers in your subconscious mind. The next time you feel like slacking, your mind reminds you of that intention, then. We simply need to hear what our minds are trying to say. Hope you now get as to why those three questions I used to ask my bosses are critical to your performance? You will stun your line manager. I can still remember the look on my line managers face when I first asked these and the comment he made. He said, "Next time I better do my homework before I have the performance review meeting with you"

Corporate Objectives

Consider a situation of a single mother who was fired from her job but has to feed her two children? She would be anxious, tired, scared, and overwhelmed of how she will survive the future which leads to self-doubt. This self-doubt pushes her to make bad decisions or to stop trying. These decisions that she makes can bury her, until she comes to a point where she pauses to think, 'How am I going to better this?' A simple goal she can have in her life is to "educate her children". That goal is enough to change her mind completely. She can give the children a better life than she ever did, and to make that goal a reality, she can wake up to meet a daily objective on time without an alarm, driven by a purpose to do every day something towards educating her children. This goal will result in a hardworking yet proud mother. That is how powerful a goal can be. It can change a life

Corporates driven by compelling goals and ruthless execution are the ones which thrive. We pretty much know that the difference between a goal and an objective is that a goal is a definition of where a company aims to be in the future and the objectives help the company to achieve it. However, most of us tend to develop objectives that are not aligned to corporate or at a granular level to departmental or branch objectives. The key to better performance year on year is to know the granular objective of the company and to also have personal objectives.

Let me give a simple example from a banking perspective. Let's say you are attached to a branch which has an objective of growing the deposit base and you are part of the deposit mobilisation team. Now, as a young executive what *Skills, Attitude, Knowledge and Environmental Understanding* should you have that will impact your role performance? You will obviously need to be able to sell, but do you know what to sell? I, often in my strategic planning secessions, ask people, "What the company is selling"? Trust me, I get different answers. Mercedes is not selling cars, they are selling prestige. So therefore you need to know what to sell, "Is it the stability of the bank, competitive interest rates, convenience of banking, access to a range of other products, and your personalised service!"

What knowledge should you have? Competitors' interest rates, the number of banks in the area and possibly the deposit bases, who the high net worth customers are, the industries in the area and demographic details. What attitudes should you have? Perseverance, "must do" mind-set and not to give up or be discouraged. And finally what are the environmental factors you think are important for you to perform your role? Externally, the dominant industries in the area. If it is an agricultural area, then you need to know the main crops, market prices and the seasons. This knowledge will tell you the timings of excess cash in the area. This approach of sharpening the role influences to align to the company's objectives and is applicable for any industry as all business are selling either a service or a product and you will see how you will breakaway and standout from the pack.

Getting aligned to corporate objectives without diagnosing your role would not take you anywhere. You have to be able to identify the role influencers if you are to convert behaviour to performance. Then your mind has to be activated to achieve them. The significance of setting objectives in any situation is that your brain signals to you of your objective and it helps you to think clearer. Then, during any obstacle that you face, your mind will overpower any obstacle you are facing because of the objective you have set and which you are determined to achieve. This determination is what helps you. When you accept a role, you are given several business objectives to achieve. Along with this objective, you can create an objective in your mind that suits the role on leading your team, what you are going to achieve for yourself, your team and the business. These objectives will help you perform.

These simple objectives will contribute to developing yourself which is key in a career. It will help achieve your purpose whilst helping to achieve the expected outcome of the company's. We have to take a moment to think how the role contributes to your personal development. It is only then you will be activated to cross the line from behaviour to performance

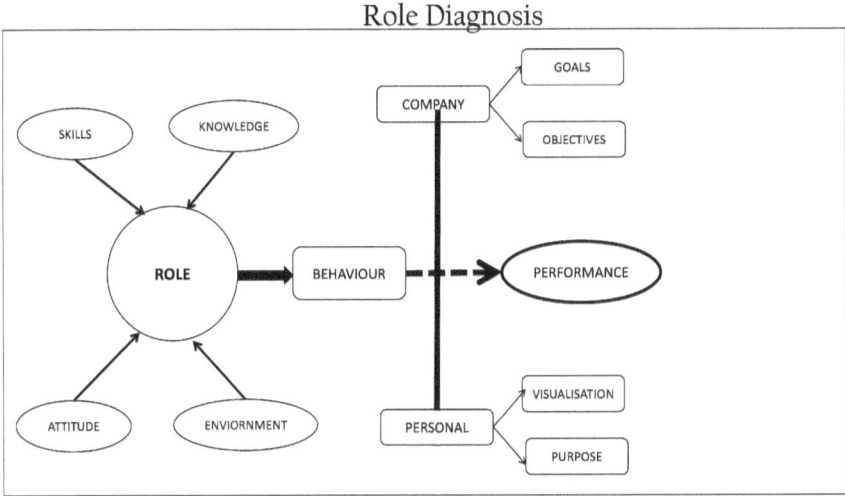

Fig. 8

Seven

PERFORMANCE

*"Winners don't do different things. They do
thing differently" – Shiv Khera*

Two sculptors were carving on two large pieces of stones. A person walking by asked both of them what they were up to. One said in agitation, "Can't you see I am carving a statue"? Taken aback the passer-by looked at the other. The other smilingly said, "I am creating a civilisation". Performance peaks when the doer takes pride in what he is doing. This is something we can and should inculcate in our little children even with their school work. When we take pride in what we do, our roles become purposeful and come to life.

It is very rare that we reach our highest potential without a purpose in life. Whether it be a teacher or an entrepreneur, we remain engaged during the tough times when we have a reason to. With our purpose in mind, the role that we play is the key to taking a step forward. However, our visualisation designs how we play the role that determines how large each step is. Performance in a role is significant in defining success. The efforts that you directed towards playing your role will be measured via the outcome. An organization's success depends on the collective performance of employees. Company's performance will be measured based on the financial objectives, market share, shareholder funds, so on and so forth. These indicators we know are not necessarily the ones that drive our personal performance. If you are a manager of a bank branch, you will be driven by branch profits, market share in deposit and advances and probably to be the best branch in the region. There are roles where the outputs are measurable, but there are also many, where the outputs are qualitative and in such instances you would never know where you would be placed.

For example, when an employee provides an exemplary customer service, the customer tends to rate their experience positively and this word spreads, thus creating a good reputation for the company. Performance therefore is personal. But the question is was it done because you visualised the experience you have decided to create for each and every customer interaction or was it because you thought your purpose was to delight every customer? For this step, you have to assume that you would not receive anything from your life that you didn't achieve. This simple assumption will stop you from expecting others to recognize you or people to help you out. At the end of the day, you are for yourself as everyone in the company is in competition. Companies are in competition, nations are in competition. Compete we must, for it brings out not who we are but who we could become. It is you who have to work hard to discover your potential, improve yourself and once that is done rest is self-motivation. Once you visualise the outcome of your performance and when the outcome matches the visual set in your mind, it will give you self-satisfaction like no other. It is like an artist who visualises the picture before he even touches the brush, and every stroke thereafter is as per the visual in your mind, and you rate your performance of painting that picture in comparison to the visual in your mind. This is how you put up a stunning performance on your role.

Performance is often misunderstood as being competent. Even though you may be competent at a job, it does not mean you will be a high performer. This is because even though the person is qualified for the role and has the necessary knowledge for it, he might have difficulty in execution. Real competence is "knowing how to and having the confidence to bring it to life". An employee with lesser qualifications might perform better than the highly qualified one. Therefore, an employer should not be quick to judge while an employee should not get demotivated because another person is more educated than you. Your hard work might just prove to outweigh the other.

An amateur photographer would constantly find ways to refresh his style and be different from the others. This is how he becomes better at it for his self-satisfaction. Creativity is the key to performance. Likewise, with the skills that you possess and a clear understanding of the role, you can find, is the key to performing your role. It can be as simple as your knack with words or a good memory, piled up with hard work and the determination to succeed at what you do; you are sure to improve your performance.

A salesman is usually described as a deceptive extrovert. However, what we fail to notice is that it takes hours to plan every word that they tell you. A salesman has to establish a relationship with the customer and persuade him to buy his product within a matter of minutes. It isn't easy as it looks, out of the hundred attempts he makes, a maximum of just two will say yes. His performance depends on how eloquently he can speak to the customers to persuade them that they desire the product. It requires a great deal of hard work to improve performance. "Practice makes perfect". Performance can be achieved by practice. Practice will help you understand your role better and once your mind gets the hang of it, it begins to think of ways to do it differently. You tend to do a bit more than what is required and this helps you to do a higher quality job.

None of us are "born to succeed or to fail." Similarly, none of us are great performers at the start. Of course some of us get a head start in life while some have to plough through which makes it that much more interesting. *Defining your role based on the acquisition of particular skills, knowledge, and attitude and understanding the environment you are in, fuelled by the purposeful visualisation delivers performance.* If you remember this line, and only this line from the entire book it is worth your investment.

Move away from the notion of, "the environment I work to is the environment I compete in'. When you think "competition", you begin to work on yourself and become competitive with yourself and better the performance progressively.

Performance and focus are related. Usain Bolt says "distraction of a Nano second will cost you the race". I remember when Robin Sharma came to Sri Lanka I had the privilege of spending personal time with him because I was the Director of the company that brought him to Colombo. Robin wanted what he called the "green room" where he spent least two hours before the presentation all by himself without any interruption. When I was taking him to the airport I asked him about the "green room concept"? Robin very kindly said, "Bradley, I rehearse my entire presentation in my mind as many times as possible. And recall the mistakes that occurred during the previous presentation. It may be my 100th show but I mentally prepare as if it is my maiden show". That left a lasting lesson in me and ever since then, I did the same with all my presentations. Preparation delivers performance – for that matter, for <u>everything</u> within a day's work. We are so unprepared for the day. Nonetheless we believe at the end of the day we have performed.

Let's see what happens in a day's work. We are woken up by a smart phone alarm, when we are not prepared to wake. We then dive in to the routine, get to office and see what's up for the day, like we ask, "What's for breakfast?" Sometime in my mid-career I made it a habit, I would ask my PA at mid-day what's my "diary" for the next day? (This was before the smart phone era). I would then spend the last hour or two preparing for the next day and briefing others who need to join the meetings. This way you are prepared to perform the next day. And guess what, during the drive to work I just run through the day's activity list to the detail of framing some of the opening comments for the meetings. It's like getting in to the "green room" every day before you step out to perform on your "work stage".

Role performance is a combination of effectiveness and efficiency - Doing the right things right. This means a daily reinforcement of what is expected of your role, for the company/ unit and for yourself. By now you would have realized that understanding the role is crucial for performance. Once you understand that and practise the daily "green room" ritual, your subconscious mind will make it a routine to shape your abilities for the day, steering you in the right direction to meet the goals. Remember this line from Shiv Khera, *"Winners don't do different things. They do things differently"*. To do things differently, on a daily basis, you need to prepare on a daily basis.

Eight

"PERFORMANCE ROI"

"The highest levels of performance come to people who are centred, intuitive, creative, and reflective – people who know to see a problem as an opportunity" – Deepak Chopra

Be it work or another engagement, it is human nature to expect appreciation. Even the dog that brings a ball back to you gets the pat on his head, so is it with the horse that wins a race. Or for that matter, our heroine (we have forgotten her by now) cooks a meal, lays the dinner table, and expects an appreciation at least with an Mmmmmm! We are also so. From our childhood we look for appreciation. When it comes to work, it is the same. We have often felt that we are not appreciated, not recognized. I have heard many people complain. I must confess that I too up to a point of time in my career felt demotivated, when some others (in my view), have contributed less but are better recognized. More often we feel some are favoured. These situations are as we see them, and will continue to appear. When such things happen people slow down, reduce enthusiasm and talk negatively. I have gone through the same until I came to realize, that I cannot change what happens in companies, but I can change the way I react to such a situation. I realized negative behaviour was self-destructive and I would be the eventual looser.

It is this my realisation that I have brought in as the personal visualisation and purpose to the equation. When I focus primarily on my purpose and visualise my future position, I began to realize that one lower increment or the delay in a promotion became insignificant. I decided to raise my bar for my own performance and regardless of what the company rewarded me, I was performing better year on year. When we do this we will make the management feel guilty.

The perception of career progress is built around increments, promotions, perks, foreign training, more responsibility and more power. These are all feel good factors and what I call the *"Outside In"* impact. All these are dependent on external views or mercies which are beyond our control. Are these not expectations we create for ourselves, based on our own judgement of our performance and how historically others have been rewarded or recognised? And as I mentioned earlier, when our expectations are not met we dilute ourselves. Why worry of matters that are beyond our control? I am going to, in the next five chapters, to share with you a completely different perspective. But I can guarantee, if you adopt my approach, nothing will slow you down.

Role Diagnosis

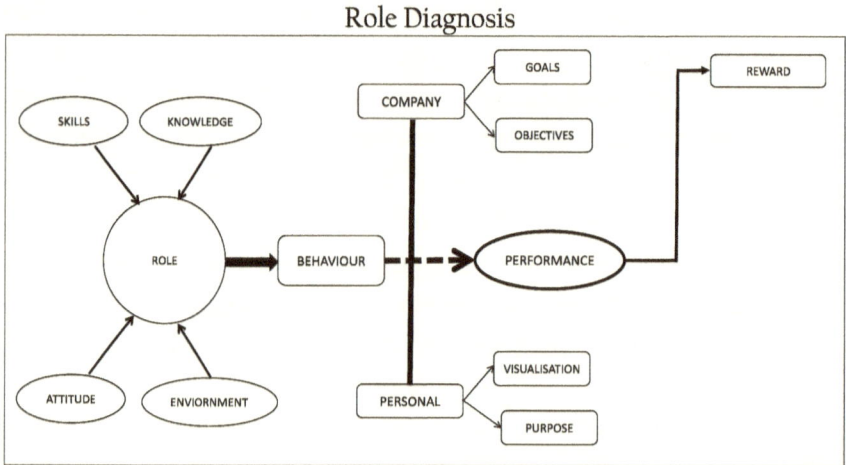

Fig. 9

Nine

REWARD

"No person was ever honoured for what he received. Honour has been the reward for what he gave".
- Calvin Coolidge

Any employee working for an organization performs well with certain expectations of a reward in his or her mind. He/she works hard to achieve certain benefits in return, for their personal satisfaction. The most common cliché assumption that we make when we work for an organization is that we would get recognized for our performance. In most cases, businesses do reward employees for their performance provided it contributes significantly to the corporate objectives and goals. However, most of them have a criterion such as a target to be achieved to be rewarded. It only recognizes the percentage of people who achieve this target and fails to reward the rest who still worked as hard as they can. In my view we are yet to have a robust system to appraise and reward every employee. But as the status quo stands, this results in employees who do "their best" to achieve the target given, but fails to do so, are further discouraged to try again. The fact is the employees' "best" may not be good enough to meet the companies' best. In a number of appraisal meetings I have heard people say I am doing my best. My response to them has been, "Do something different." Employees have expectations of being highly rewarded for their performance. The problem is that this is subjective on who and how performance is reviewed. Several problems can arise with this bias and envy. We live in a world where a high performer is always viewed by others as a threat to them. But we also live in a world where your passion could give you the courage to surpass every obstacle that you will face, a world where the most impossible dreams can come true. Yet reward may not be what you expected and when you expected.

There is always a problem with non-rewarding and under-rewarding. We often think highly of ourselves when we achieve something in our role. Even if we are rewarded for our achievements, we feel that we deserve more as we tend to compare the rewards given to others and end up being unsatisfied about the reward we received. There will always be a gap based on comparison and negativity in the rewarding system. We expect higher rewards which create a level of stress because what we want is not what we get. This will hinder your performance.

How will you overcome this? Careers are very long journeys. You will not necessarily be stuck in one company or department. The biggest myth that is harming performance is that you are performing for the employer. The fact that performance benefits the employer is true. However, non recognition of your performance is more harmful to yourself. Set aside external factors and think of how improving your performance for your sake will benefit you. Each little achievement you self-recognise brings you a step forward to shaping you, hardening your metal. Happiness within yourself is above all. It overweighs all material rewards and validation from your peers and boss.

Like I mentioned above, the most cliché assumption that we make is that we will get something back from the organization. But that something is often combatively less than what we expected. I believe that it is in our own hands to encourage ourselves for the sake of our journey. It is like a marathon runner slowing down because

Role

the bystanders have done cheering him along the way. Therefore I want to bring you to the concept of "Self-Rewarding". Self-rewarding will motivate you to achieve your goals. Self-rewards are ubiquitous and encouraging. What do I mean by self-rewarding? Whenever you accomplish a task, which in your mind gives you a sense of accomplishment, then you need to be rewarded. Tell yourself, "Well Done …. (your name); give yourself a thumbs-up, a YES; cross your arm, pat your shoulder and tell yourself, "You did it." Also, share it with your closest friend or your spouse as soon as the task is done. Honour yourself with little rewards like as above, no matter how small the achievement is without waiting for your boss or company to recognize it days, weeks or months later. Remember, every little accomplishment you give yourself accumulates and keeps you encouraged. Effectively, it also keeps you in shape emotionally. You know how very emotionally down you have felt after an annual review, or when you were left out of the list of new promotees?

When I was in the management of Nations Trust Bank, Priyantha Talwatte, a close friend and colleague once said to me, "Brad, the management level is a lonely place, and you have to pat yourself and move on". The corporate management level is like a race where everyone is competing to reach the pinnacle. Your fellow runners would not pause to appreciate your speed or your hard work. They would not congratulate you, but would rather focus on them reaching closer to the finish line because it means you will be overtaken. So, I learnt that when I win a "lap" to pat my own back and keep running. This way I never got emotionally burdened to be slowed down. Nations Trust Bank is one of the very aggressive JKH companies. (JKH is among the top three companies in Sri Lanka). Everyone in the corporate management team was a CEO prospect. One can imagine the energy and competitiveness in that team. It is at Nations Trust Bank that I found my metal.

Neither the world nor the company you work for, owe you anything. You should not expect others to respect and reward you.

The only person who owes you anything is yourself. It is what you earn and not what others give you is what is important. So why should you expect others to honour you for it? Pamper yourself with self-rewards, take a day off. Give your family a treat. Simple things bring happiness within you that is beyond any other reward you receive. You have the most power to motivate yourself- make use of the power.

Role Diagnosis

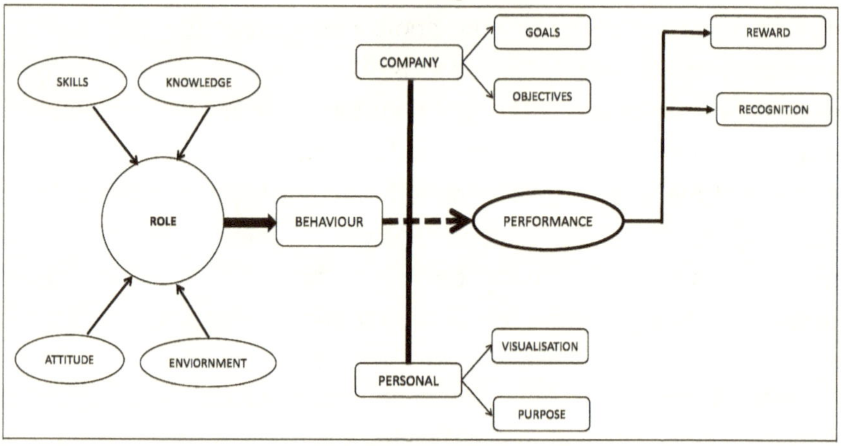

Fig. 10

Ten

RECOGNITION

"Don't worry when you not recognized, bur strive to be worthy of recognition". – Abraham Lincoln

We depend on others- for acceptance, validation, recognition, help, motivation and encouragement and often end up with disappointment. Similarly, employees expect the employers to do the same, comparative to how colleagues are recognized. People, we must accept, are influenced by own beliefs, perceptions and another's opinion- it is human nature. We are often drowned by criticism and by the judgement of others. Drowning is not the intent, swimming is the intent. Remember Finding Nimo (hope you've seen the movie, if not please watch) where Dory, the Blue Tang, goes "Keep on swimming." This got all the other fishes in the net saying to themselves "keep on swimming" until they collectively broke the line, brought the net down, and escaped.

I learnt to see others criticisms as their own weakness. I learnt to recognize my genuine efforts even though I may fall short of the expected outcome. We work more for "You are great" than "Great effort". Why do we depend on others for recognition? It may come or, maybe not, when it was rightfully due, or, not at all. Instead, let's disregard this demoralizing expectation. As I have suggested in the previous chapter, focus on your long term purpose. See every position that you hold as an opportunity. Make yourself worthy of your own recognition. In this context challenge yourselves to perform to your true potential, regardless of whether we are noticed for it or given recognition; because at the end of the day we gain the most from our performance. It is not that you are not noticed, but ignored due to the inadequacies of the system, and if you slow down due to the absence of being noticed, you are submitting to the inadequacies of others. But if you continue to act positively; your colleagues are likely to support you, subordinates are likely to respect you and your superiors might finally realize your efforts and recognize you, or yet, maybe not.

But why would you want to spend your time and perform for simply the "maybe's" and "could be's"?

Why would you get discouraged because you did not receive good comments from others? Why would you want to slow down because you think you deserve validation which you didn't get?

Nonetheless, my mantra to you is go on regardless….as long as your inner self in not ashamed of you.

Give recognition to every effort of others – your peers, superiors, team members, for every little thing they have done that has contributed to you looking good, even if it's only to you, *yourself and not to your superiors.*

It is like the time we spend in front of the mirror and we step away only when we look good for ourselves. If someone comments positively on your looks, well and good, but you don't wait to start your day until someone make a positive comment on your looks.

We seldom realize that we perform below potential in every position we hold in our entire careers. Ask yourself, if you have thus far had the best in your career? Don't we have those after thoughts that "goes," "I could have done it better"? This is my point, when we know deep inside that we could have done better, why expect someone to recognize your half self? Having said that, consider the psyche's need of appreciation of which you know yourself the best?

If you analyse yourself and your position based on who you are, you might just realize that you are capable of doing much better. Therefore, it is important to judge yourself before taking into consideration other's judgements. You have diagnosed your role and you have defined what performance will shape you for a better you. Therefore, every accomplishment that shapes you needs to be recognized. Recognized by you.

It does not matter what the others think of how you perform. Only your determination would make it through to the end. Only you can define your role. You are able to challenge yourself to play your role in a much different way which you believe would prove to be successful to achieve the objectives.

Cricket is a famous game in Sri Lanka. Think of a cricketer who is not recognized for his performance. Papers avoid writing about his scores and he is discouraged by it. He feels the need to give up. However, if he takes this approach he would think to himself that even if he stops scoring, the paper would not lose. His journey would stop because of an external influence: How the media thinks of him. So, what he has to do is to disregard this, pat his back to motivate himself and continue scoring. Who knows, the papers might just recognize his motivation. If that was you, I would suggest, Go, gift yourself a new bat. "I have done this for myself. I have just ordered a cake for my team". Not saying why. The purpose is to reward myself with a joy of a celebration.

How do you recognize yourself? What is the recognition you believe in? You want your name to be known. From now or you want to leave a legacy. If you are to leave a legacy, you can, no matter the time you have spent in a department. Take a game of soccer for example. The game is of ninety minutes duration. But a single player would handle the ball for about only four minutes. And in that four minutes that one player will bring out a moment that may not only make a change to the game but leave a lasting memory for him and to the spectator. In such a scenario what is his recognition? Scaling up his personal capabilities and enhancing his marketability!

The best reward you can give yourself is to scale up your marketability. When you have this focus within yourself, it would not matter whether you are recognized. It will be about getting the job done as a team and as a department. You would not need personal recognition, but you need to encourage yourself with self-recognition. You have to take it into your mind to do it yourself. How many times have you been amazed at what you have done, your capabilities and your performance? This "wow" factor comes within yourself- you will not get it from others. The moment you recognize yourself- you're gearing yourself up to the next level. When you achieve something brilliant, isn't it satisfying to simply think of how much of effort and hard work you put to it and to see it finally being achieved? I don't think there is any more satisfaction than seeing yourself prosper, seeing yourself accomplish and achieve. This is what you must know. Recognizing yourself is far more valuable and satisfying than being recognized by another, because at the end of the day it is you who knows yourself best.

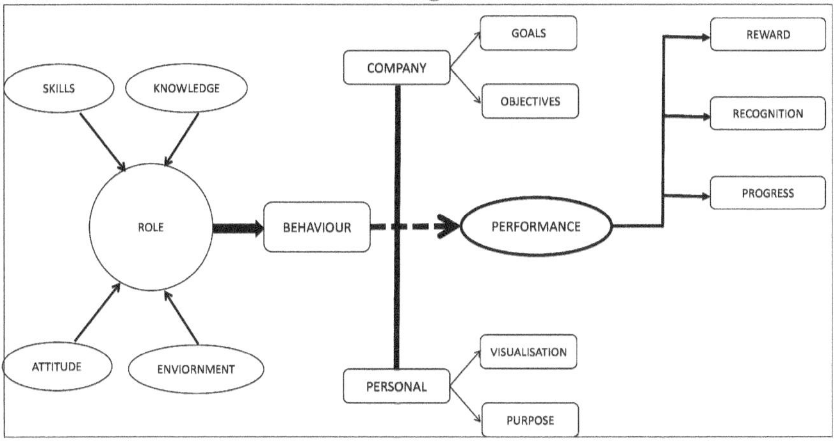

Fig. 11

Eleven

PROGRESS

> *"Progress is impossible without change, and those who cannot change their mind cannot change anything"* - George Bernard Shaw

Progress is when you achieve a milestone in your life journey. It is not just when you catch another star in the universe on your way to the moon. It has to have relevance to the company (or the unit you are in) and more importantly to your purpose. In a career, we believe that a milestone is when we get that promotion you have been working for or getting selected as employee of the month. We classify progress with advancement in position. In a layman's personal life, success could be measured by the acquisition of assets, completing a professional qualification or Master's degree.

Nonetheless, we generally fail to see the bigger picture. I think of it in the perspective of your (higher) purpose. What is progress in relation to your purpose in a particular role when you have a higher purpose? It is when you work towards improving your capabilities and competencies. Once you have understood your role, diagnosed on how best you can perform it and identified the skills and competencies you can use in this job role, you have to make it a reality by making it happen.

Your focus and visualisation determines your reality. When you are focused on enhancing yourself, you progress. Once again I am self-centring the approach to your expectations. Annual appraisals are more looking back and less looking forward. In my view a company may have progression plans for a few. As we all know organisations are like pyramids, the higher it goes the narrower it gets.

We often misjudge the appraisals and the resulting increments as measurements of progress for ourselves. There could be financial benefits, or maybe even a promotion, but is it real progress? Nonetheless, do you ever stop to think, of your idea, on the progress you have made?

It is crucial to analyse yourself and your improvements. What progress have I made during the course of the year? Think of a day that you made someone else smile because of something you did for them? Have you impacted anyone's life? Think, even of mundane things like, "Have you eaten 'healthy'?" Have you met new people? Have you forgiven others? Have you travelled and learnt new things? Have you completed an extraordinary task during the year?

Real progress is not limited to whether you got the promotion or which car you bought this year. We do not live simply for ourselves. It is important to live a balanced life, and if you have lived this year a lot better than last year, that is when you have made progress. But how will this balanced life connect with your performance? Good advice is usually when someone says to aim high and do great things, but I always think that a slight variation in this would benefit us in our everyday lives. Take small steps to achieve the big things. Little things such as helping another and making your parents smile are important to progress in life. This will also help you progress in your thinking and you begin to focus on your own progress rather than burdening your mind with things that weigh you down such as envy, negativity and hatred.

Role

Being positive and focusing on energizing yourself will increase your capacity and this will help in your betterment. You will confidently raise your hand to take up the more difficult things in your role because you have progressed in your capacity.

This is far more sustainable. It will improve your intellectual capacity, your competency, wisdom, inter-personal skills and lead you to self-realisation. You have then passed all the narrow paths and progressed to a wider freeway. No doubt, this is the best way you can progress in your performance.

How do you know that you have progressed? Ask yourself whether you have moved closer to the person you visualised in your role? Do an appraisal comparing to what you are, to what you visualised to be when you accepted the role. Your visualization is the optimum target to achieve and once you set your mind to it, you will not be discouraged by petty opinions. One of the main reasons people fail to reach their potential is because they live the life prescribed by other's judgements or measures.

They say you are confined only by the walls you build yourself. So, break those walls in your mind and strengthen your mind through determination. *As per the quote by George Bernard Shaw, "Progress is only possible when there is a change in the mind-set."* Only you can assess your progress and only you have the ability to improve it, as long as you do not give up, but keep on moving forward.

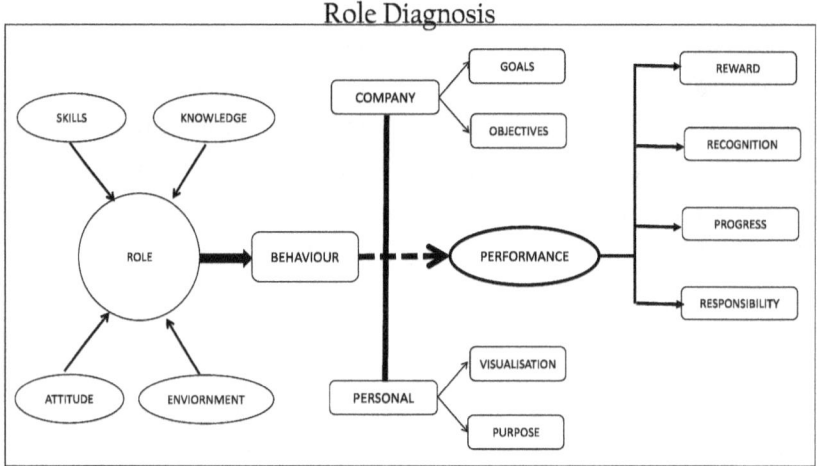

Fig. 12

Twelve
RESPONSIBILITY

"In the long run, we shape our lives, and we shape ourselves. The process never ends until we die. And the choices we make are, ultimately our own responsibility." –Eleanor Roosevelt

As the saying goes opportunity is not something that would knock on your door by itself, and we know it is something that we need to be alert to capture or create it ourselves. We often limit ourselves to the JD – the "Job Description" or the career prescription.

JD becomes your defence fence to protect you from taking additional responsibility. I have had people working with me say to me that an assignment that I gave was not in their JD. The answer, however, was simple. I amended the JD and told them "It is now...". The point I want to make here is that more responsibilities we voluntarily take outside our JD exposes our versatility and widens your horizon. Let me share with you one of my personal experiences. When I joined CIMA in May 2007 my designation was CEO Sri Lankan Division, and my JD was limited to Sri Lanka. When reviewing the presence of Sri Lankan members across the world, I realised that there were quite a number of CIMA members in the Maldives. This prompted me to seek an opportunity to teach CIMA in the Maldives. I reached out through a phone call to a business school in Male. Fortunately its Head of Education Dr Anwar was the former

Minister of Education. And through him we signed an agreement with the Maldivian Ministry of Education to sponsor 50 students to study CIMA. Now this was outside my JD.

But by doing this I was able to show that I am capable of growing markets outside Sri Lanka. This made my boss look good and he gave me an open mandate to explore possibilities of expansion in other areas of South Asia. That's how I set my path to unconnectedly becoming the Regional Director. One act outside the JD, one self-imposed responsibility, outcome of diagnosing the role and visualising my purpose in the role, reaped dividends.

Taking the initiative to present an innovative idea or leading a team when needed, these scenarios of taking matters into your own hands represents "self-responsibility". We expect responsibilities to be given to us as a recognition for performance. But responsibilities accrue not out of performance but more out of personal capabilities. Responsibilities are given to those who demonstrate that they can take responsibilities. We are able to create our own opportunities to be responsible, when we have diagnosed the role and visualised our purpose in the role. It is then that we are recognized as being able to take responsibility.

The things that you are not comfortable of are however the ones connected to your purpose of reaching for the stars. Being confident enough to dare yourself by doing things that others would be hesitant to do is one way that you can take more responsibility. This is when you visualize who you want to become and work towards it. This makes you a responsible person as your inner capacity progresses. Everyone is born with the ability to acquire the talent and skill within themselves. Those who identify and exploit this are the ones who succeed in any role that they perform. That's responsibility!

Role Diagnosis

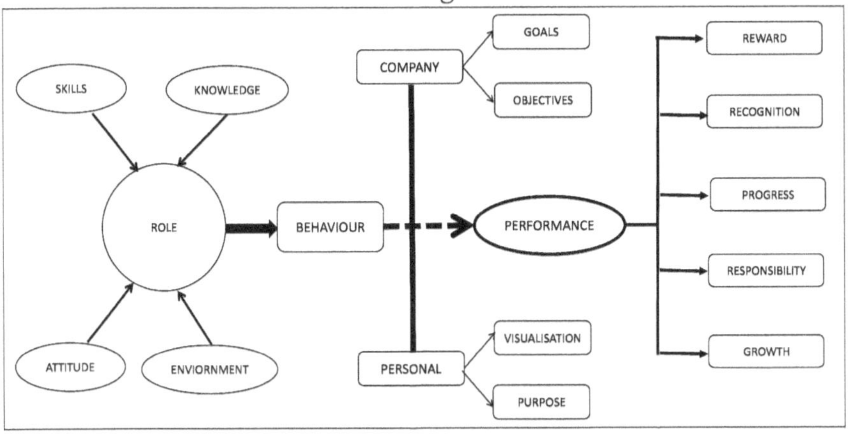

Fig. 13

Thirteen

GROWTH

"What you habitually think largely determines what you ultimately become" – Bruce lee

Have you ever had moments where you were overwhelmed at what you accomplished and your unconscious minds saying out loud, 'I can't believe I did this!' How many times so far in your life have you done this? I feel this every time I look at my "Tips in Ten" short episodes in my YouTube channel. Same feeling when I look at my MBA dissertation. I felt the same reading the final script of this book. I cannot possibly imagine that I pulled through and did a marvellous job. ("Pat on my back!").

This is because I did not let insignificant factors push me down. I believed and I carried through till I achieved the goal. We are braver and more capable than we think we are. We simply need to take a deep breath and step outside the limitations others have imposed on us. We need to constantly hold high our purposes, separating those from the prejudices.

There is a distinct difference between career development and growth in the career. Development shows how you move up the vertical ladder in your career path. In contrast, growth in career is about how your capabilities grow. It is important to have a balance of both because it is not always about promotions and taking up higher responsibilities. It's more about improving one's learning – new knowledge and new skills, improving competencies and being ready for more difficult tasks.

In this time and age there is free access to new knowledge at our fingertips. If we only spend 10% of the time we spend on our social media space seeking such knowledge, we will be growing in competence. Organisations are focused on growth, and if you are not, you will be left behind.

Growth in your career is about increasing your capacity. The best example that can be taken is when you are amazed at your capabilities. What does this show us? There is a potential inside of us which we are not consciously building on. We deliver an outstanding output, say with our dissertation, and "leave it behind" instead of accumulating.

People who have grown in their careers are those who have consciously accumulated their accomplishments. We did not realize that we are capable of performing at such a level. We tend to underestimate ourselves. However, we are more capable of achieving much more than what we think we can based upon our human judgement. This is where the "wow" factor comes into play. From within, when you realize that you have expanded your capacity and you are now confident to raise your own bar, like what Olympians do, you improve your own standards, similar to Olympians, even if they were defeated at the event. This is growth.

It is expansion from within. Self-recognition, self-rewarding and self-activation help you navigate your thinking better, this will help you grow. Growth is saying "I can carry more weight". It is realizing that you are braver than you think, and you grow towards the person who you have visualized yourself to be, you grow towards excellence.

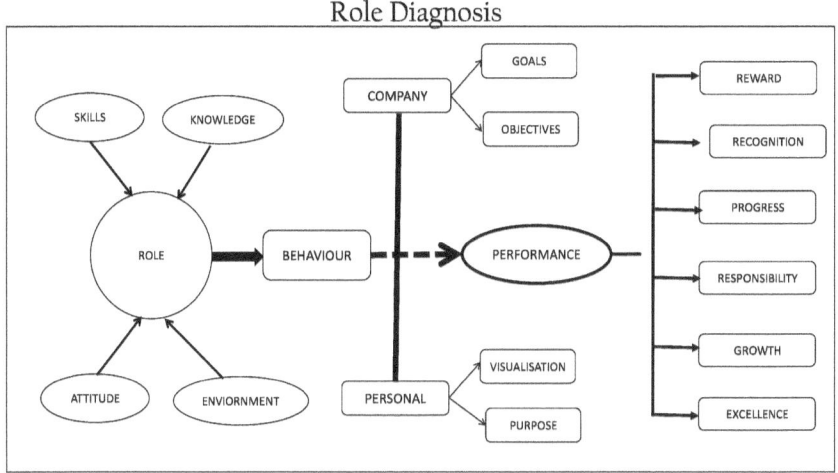

Fig. 14

Fourteen

EXCELLENCE

"The will to win, the desire to succeed, the urge to reach your full potential...these are the keys that will unlock the door to personal excellence".– Confucius

Excellence in different roles is measured in different ways. But to the one in the role excellence would mean pretty much the same. It is not exhibitionism, but it's the bravery with how you deal with your vulnerability. All Blacks of New Zeeland is the legendary rugby team in the world. Jock Hobbs, former All Blacks captain was quoted saying, "The great thing about being an All Black is that you get up every day and try to be the best in the world. That's what we're trying to do; you are getting up every morning to be the best in the world." When you wake up with a higher purpose like this, you are subconsciously activated towards excellence. Recall how you wake up, and what do you tell yourself? All these set the tone at the top of each day. Excellence has to be personal and it is only then that you can visualise.

You may have a goal of starting your own company, or of become a CEO of another's company, but run towards achieving it 'excellently' as per your convictions. On a diagnostic note, excellence is when you set ablaze the place you are in, no matter what your position is. It is like the Jamaican 4X100 relay team at the Olympics. No matter what the position of the third lapper is, when Bolt takes the baton the stadium is set ablaze. That's excellence in action. "Excellence" is when you reach your maximum potential at a given time. Reaching the maximum potential is an infinite statement. You ask the most accomplished person of this legacy? He or she is likely to say, 'I could have done better'. Therefore, true excellence will depend on the level of expectation we place on our personal potential and only that person will feel it.

Another person's definition of excellence is not valid for you, because they do not know the hours of effort that you have put in to achieve your goal. If you ask two people to give their opinion of what excellence is, each will be unique and different. When your mind thinks of excellence, it reflects on what you have achieved and what it takes to achieve your goals that you aim to achieve in the future. It develops a scenario where you become what you have visualized at the beginning of the role and what you expect to be.

How do you motivate yourself towards excellence? You have to let go of other focuses and forget about your background and past when you enter your office. Leave the baggage behind. Imagine your office is a movie set where everyone works together to create one amazing product? Maslow's hierarchy of needs outlines the need for self-actualization. This is when you have achieved "esteem needs" and "needs of belonging".

I believe we cannot reach excellence if we are burdened by not satisfying all these needs. Self-actualization to me is a journey towards my full potential (yet unknown). But this cannot be achieved without nurturing yourself, growth, without being a competent and responsible.

Genuine passion towards your role regardless of how the company compensated you is what will help you find the path towards excellence.

Is excellence simply trying to maintain what has been done before or outdoing a standard that has been set by others? No one decides what excellence is for anyone or a group of people. Excellence is when you visualize and begin to shape and form yourself to achieve it. This is pursuit of excellence. It is our minds that we have to set to achieve excellence. Our brains have a capacity to envision excellence and steer our body towards it. The journey involves growth, responsibility, self-rewarding and recognition are determined by your vision, role understanding and your higher purpose. We learn through our daily journeys and ultimately, we are able to achieve our form of excellence.

However, if you let yourself down by external judgements, prescriptions and opinions, your visualization will disappear and you will lose your purpose.

What do you expect from a company at the end of the year? Promotion, responsibility, rewards and recognition! This is the usual expectation in return to performance. But I am letting you envision a different picture; a different perspective. This is because everything mentioned above are what you expect from the company. They are an outward looking in and these are subjective. You cannot slowdown in your journey. Then you miss out the best part; the journey towards excellence.

I remember my athletic coach saying in a marathon, you do not have to lead the pack but conserve the energy for the final 200 metres. Till then just be behind the leader and let him hear your footsteps, your heavy breaths and this will stress him and slow him down. This is because he will be burdened by the fear of defeat and his mind will weaken. Your performance in any role, your success in just about anything is determined by the strength of your mind. It is up to you to strengthen your mind, and once this is done, it will guide your body to be just the same. Excellence is created by your mind and achieved by the mind. It is personal and an "inside, looking out" approach.

Conclusion

VISUALISE – RITUALISE – ACTUALISE

One of the Usain Bolt's quotes in Brainy Quotes goes like this. "When I was younger, I always wanted to impress, to be good for my country, to make them feel good and sometimes that meant I didn't focus on myself enough. I learned I had to put myself first. And it's fine because I want for me the same thing that they want for me, which is to win". This quote demonstrates a shift from "outside looking in" to and "inside looking out" and perfectly summarises my effort in this book. I had wasted a good half of my work like trying to impress and do good for the company, and when I was around 35, I realized that the company also wants me to perform. I then began to focus on my purpose and accelerated my career to such an extent that I even overtook the companies I was working for. This resulted in my changing jobs three times in seven years with position elevations.

The conclusive message for you is to set out from the myth of company focus to self-focus. Companies want you to raise your bar on your own. In fact only you will know within you how high you can raise the bar. Ask yourself what percentage of your capacity or potential is utilised by the company? Is it not less than about 70% and the company is happy with it? What happens to you? Are you not living a fake life cheating your own potential?

This makes you barren and you will lose your self-worth. So apply the model I have given you every time you change the job.

Diagnose the role. Share this with your team members during the annual objective setting meeting and help them too to diagnose their role, and guide them to perform for self-glory.

If everyone in your team is expanding their potential, your unit will be shining,

> *Purpose of life is not to live as who you are.*
> *But to be, "who you can become"*

Reviews

"There are two things we can say with certainty about the future: it will be different, and it will surprise. Now, more than ever, employees at all levels have to navigate unfamiliar, challenging times, a quickening pace of change, increasing expectations, and a rising tide of rapidly-evolving conditions. I highly recommend this book as it provides a Framework on 'Role – A Diagnostic approach to Performance' for every role or job position to ensure individual career success by examining the critical elements will impact 'performance' from both the perspective of the employer (organization) and the employee".

- Prof Sattar Bawany,
Chairman & CEO, Centre for Executive Education (CEE Global)
& Strategic Advisor, International Professional Managers
Association (IPMA UK)

"An excellent guide to taking charge of your own destiny, both in your career and personal aspirations. A vital handbook which would assist in driving performance through individual ownership".

- Surani Amerasinghe
Head of Human Resources
Lion Breweries PLC, Sri Lanka

It is a novel handbook for management practitioners with multiple hats that commendably guides on diagnosing their and that of their teams' roles for harnessing excellence in performance in organizational and personal affairs turning this challenge into a simple, precise and achievable practice. This book remarkably integrates and simplifies necessary concepts that managers need to incorporate in routine exercise for paving success towards targeted achievements, goals and self-glory. A commendable knowledge guide for managers with multiple portfolios!

- Dr. Qaisar Abbas
Professor of HRD and Director COMSATS University, Lahore, Pakistan

"This is a must read book for everyone who aspires to progress and maintain control over what's important with their personal development. The Diagnostic Approach to Role breaks down winning approach to understanding any role and ace it"

-Datin Malliga Subramaniam
Certified Career Coach &
Senior Managing Partner
Shadowdata Software, Sdn, Bhd

"Doing your tasks well regardless of not being recognized by your bosses, will in the long run, help one's professional development is the theme". A number of 'out of the box' solutions are also given and explained"

- Paneetha Ameresekere
Journalist, Sri Lanka

Simple, practical and a compelling read. Having scoured through many a management and HR textbook, I picked up the manuscript with ready to retire into technical reading and purely to do the honours for a friend and professional peer. I was in for a pleasant shock. I was spellbound by the clarity, simplicity and the forthrightness of *the book. It didn't leave my hand until I got to the very end. Bradley has deftly woven decades of leadership experience into an authentic prescription to cure role related dysfunctions, a malaise that strikes many leaders, professionals and organizations today. This is an excellent read for those of us who hover the corporate world, seeking new learning and solutions. What to do and not to do as a lease is provided with practical* insights.

- L Chiranthi Cooray
DGM HR/ Chief HR Officer
Hatton National Bank PLC

With Robin Sharma

www.ingramcontent.com/pod-product-compliance
Lightning Source LLC
Chambersburg PA
CBHW030858180526
45163CB00004B/1628